Illusions

Illusions

By ANDRÉ MAUROIS

COLUMBIA UNIVERSITY PRESS

NEW YORK & LONDON 1968

The George B. Pegram Lectures

THE TRUSTEES of Associated Universities, Inc., established the annual George B. Pegram Lectureship at Brookhaven National Laboratory to provide a forum at which leaders in the fields of scholarship, research, letters and the arts, and public service could consider in depth the interaction of science, the humanities, and our society. The lectureship was named to honor George Braxton Pegram (1877–1958), one of the most influential scientists of the nuclear age. He was Professor of Physics, Dean, and Vice President of Columbia University. In 1946 he headed the Initiatory University Group which proposed that a regional center for research in the nuclear sciences be established in the New York area, and thus he played a key role in the establishment of Associated Universities, Inc., and the founding of Brookhaven National Laboratory. George B. Pegram's lucid mind and gentle ways will long be remembered by those who knew him. This series in his honor has been established to further his conviction that the results of science can be made to serve the needs and hopes of mankind.

Usually each lecture series is given over a period of about two weeks, during which time the lecturer resides at the Laboratory. In the fall of 1967 Brookhaven was anticipating such a period of interaction with the great and very human French Man of Letters, André Maurois. To our great sorrow M. Maurois' sudden fatal illness occurred immediately before his departure from France was scheduled. He had, however, prepared his manuscript for these lectures, and his family, acting through M. Gérald Maurois, has most graciously and generously sent this manuscript to us for presentation and publication.

The Laboratory was fortunate and honored that Jacques Barzun, the University Professor at Columbia University, consented to present the lectures to their intended audience and to aid in the editing of them for publication. Because of his own distinguished background in scholarship and letters and his personal acquaintance with Maurois, Professor Barzun brought clarity and perception to his presentation. We are very grateful for his efforts in our behalf and for the excellent prefatory remarks he has provided for this book.

Our appreciation goes also to M. Edouard Morot-Sir, Cultural Counselor to the French Embassy at Washington and Representative of French Universities in the United States, for his illuminating foreword in appreciation of André Maurois.

THE PEGRAM LECTURESHIP COMMITTEE

> R. Christian Anderson
> George C. Cotzias
> Orrington E. Dwyer
> Cavid Erginsoy
> William A. Higinbotham
> Ronald F. Peierls
> Thomas V. Sheehan
> Maynard E. Smith
> George M. Woodwell
> Edward V. Sayre, Chairman

Foreword by Edouard Morot-Sir

IT IS IMPOSSIBLE to evoke with words alone the personality of André Maurois. I can recall the gentle expression of his eyes, his smile, the finesse and warmth of his voice. I remember him in his study surrounded by his books, on a podium behind a lectern, at a table with some friends. Perhaps an artist would be able to bring to life his unique presence. With words, I can only suggest it. The man who wrote these lectures (which are among the last texts he wrote) was a French writer who was at once typically French, the authentic product of a history and a culture, and typically international in the wide range of his interests, the extent of his knowledge, and his sense of national and ethnic diversities. Let me say that your country had a privileged place in his heart; admiration, gratitude, and a thorough understanding which led to an unalterable friendship—these are the sentiments which André Maurois cultivated for the United States of America. And this friendship was intimately bound up with his humanism. A defender of the human values on which your country is based and from which American civilization has developed, André Maurois will remain in our powerful, creative, troubled, and cruel century the purest and most honest witness of western humanism, where this humanism ceases being western and becomes universal.

André Maurois was above all a *man of culture,* a man with

an insatiable curiosity about man. To him can be applied the saying of the Latin writer: "Nothing that is human is foreign to me." And this curiosity directed him toward the past, toward history. In the third of these lectures he says: "We must revert to the traditions which have helped men to steer their course among the reefs and shallows of life." And in another passage he describes his attitude toward the past in this way: "A man does not break away from the past of humanity any more than he frees himself of his own body." Hence this rule for moral and intellectual conduct: "A man should, to act and to live, accept the bulk of the moral, social and religious rules which humanity before him has deemed necessary." This type of dialogue with the past signifies both re-creation and judgment, an immense *work* which, through the intermediary of one man, gives humanity a consciousness of itself as a whole. This respect for work is one of the most important aspects of humanism; there is no culture without this daily effort on the part of man. In fact, André Maurois had adopted this maxim as his guiding rule: "Much work, a woman you love and loyal friends." In speaking of the success of Madame de Maintenon with King Louis the Fourteenth, and of his radiant mistress, Madame de Montespan, he concludes: "A man worthy of the name loves his work more than anything in the world, even more than the woman he loves." Culture, then, is work, and also education. For Maurois, every writer was an educator. This does not mean that he favored a didactic and always tedious literature, but he felt that the writer has, of necessity, the responsibilities of an educator. He is the cultural intermediary par excellence among men. He forms, he instructs, he is an intellectual and moral guide; and he is this inevitably, for better or for worse perhaps, but this is his vocation and he must never forget it. And this is undoubtedly why *André Maurois identified culture with order*. He said, "The horror of disorder has always been one of my strongest sentiments." Do not view this confession under a superficial light. Certainly Maurois was an organized and methodical man, with a well-ordered study and files. But to an even greater extent, the taste for order represented the exceptional convergence of truth and beauty which has been the secret of the great classical eras of antiquity as well as of modern times. Order is the intellect and the heart at once controlled, dominated, and balanced in works which then express the beauty of their truth. To quote Maurois: "Only the collaboration of reasoning, experience and action can give us, not a permanent victory which is not in the nature of things, but a moment of respite and a happy stop-over under one of these fragile shelters which are called civilizations." Order, then, is the image of every culture and the product of the assiduous work of man. It is a common value of thought, sentiment, and action, and is thus the essence of every civilization. You will have noted the modest nature of the civilizing appeal I just quoted. I perceive in it a remarkable blend of modesty and firmness, of resignation and hope. And in this sense Maurois offered us an extraordinary synthesis of skeptical and stoical attitudes; this, in my mind, is the highest form of every culture. This union of two traditions which in appearance are opposed has been present in French thought since the Renaissance. André Maurois tried in our time to make this double necessity understood: on one hand, an intelligence which knows that the last word of truth is that there are no truths, and on the other hand, an unshakable and heroic resolve which, from day to day, from century to century, is prepared to begin a new man's desperate effort to give his life meaning and order.

A man of culture, André Maurois was also an "homme d'esprit." This is a difficult phrase to translate into English because of the double meaning of the word "esprit" in French— at once mind and wit. Yes, here also we discover a curious meeting of thought and wit, which is the ultimate expression of our art of living. "Esprit" is above all courtesy, and we know that André Maurois was a man of infinite politeness. He writes: "Everything can be said with good grace, and it would indeed be a mistake to take brutality to be the only form of candor." Courtesy is understanding, kindness and humor—the kind of humor which knows how to laugh at itself and which minimizes false tragedies. And this politeness for him applied especially to the relations between man and woman. He writes, not without gentle humor: "It is a banal, but a rather exact image to compare the movement of a woman's soul with that of an ocean. The wise husband never becomes indignant. Like a sailor in a storm, he slackens the sails, waits, hopes, and the passing storms do not prevent him from loving the sea." Hence Maurois' smile (and all those who knew him remember it), a smile which meant, first of all, concern for others—not merely indulgence ready to forgive, but respect for what the other is. And there is also a politeness of thought which is linked with the ideal of order. Maurois despised excess in every form—emphasis, exaggeration, hyperbole. "The great secret," he often said, "is the natural." Here again is a notion which is delicate to analyze. The natural is the contrary of nature, and is even the extreme opposite of it. The natural is the supreme effort of art; it is art which has surmounted effort to become the ease and grace which hide the terrible tensions and contractions of the will. The natural is not the return to the good savage, but the perfectly civilized man, the man who has been able to substitute the order of culture for the order of nature. And thus we pass, via an unnoticeable and unviolent transition, from intelligence to wit, which is amusement, sport, brilliance—the free play of spontaneous thought. Maurois, man of the world, brilliant conversationalist who knew how to tell anecdotes, loved this fantasy of the intellect but he knew its limits. "It is not sufficient to have it. You must have enough of it to avoid having too much." It is typical of Maurois to use such a witticism to show the limits of wit. Is this not the epitome of a certain cultural refinement? But we must know how to go farther in this universe of courtesy where the rules of the intellect and those of society converge. "Esprit" is moderation, and moderation in all things—in the expression of thoughts and feelings, in social behavior, and especially in regard to oneself. The supreme courtesy is not taking oneself too seriously, is it not? Maurois avoided every form of vanity and conceit. And you can be assured of the sincerity of his words near the beginning of the first lecture: "What I seek to be, as I stand before you here, is an average human being who, in all good faith, is trying to understand. That and nothing more." And you see why intelligence, politeness, human relations, "esprit," and the natural are one and the same reality; that is, culture, as the crowning of every form of human civilization.

Man of culture, man of wit, André Maurois was for me, finally, *a man of tolerance and generosity.* And this rounds out his humanism. He confessed that two defects appalled him above all others. Stupidity, first of all, about which he says: "Human stupidity and malevolence at random are without limits." You will find in these words the skeptic and the ironist who, despite his unlimited tolerance, were not easily resigned to accepting the stupidity of others! And the other fault which repelled him was wickedness. At the age of seventy he wrote: "When I encountered wickedness for the first time, I was stupefied, and I still am." A moving confession coming from a man who loved people passionately in their past and in their present. He did not understand wickedness or, rather, refused to understand it, for it is the incarnation of evil, the only obstacle to the victory of intelligence, the source of all fanaticism. Tolerance is the possibility of opening indefinitely new dialogues among people. And André Maurois thought of his role as a writer in this way: a master of thought, an educator, the representative of a tradition. He was essentially an intermediary between the individuals for whom he played, and will continue to play, the roles of confidant and personal adviser; for the nations whose histories he wrote and whose temperaments he described; for the generations he tried to bring closer together.

From all this an ethic which is on man's level is derived—an ethic without pretension for grandiloquence, and made up of daily experiences and of what is called the wisdom of nations—an ethic which should help man to brave the difficulties he is confronted with each day, in this tragicomedy which is personal existence. We rediscover here the stoic and the skeptic closely associated and reconciled. In his book, *Art of Living,*

Maurois praises the common sense of Gabriel Hanotaux, who liked to offer useful precepts designed to give comfort in times of need. For example: "Everything happens. . . . Everything works out. . . . No one understands anything about anything. . . . If everyone knew what everyone else was saying about everyone, no one would speak to anyone. . . . Above all, never be afraid. The enemy who makes you retreat is afraid of you at the same time." Is this the serenity of an old man who has been through everything? No, for behind these maxims there is a very alert intelligence which never gives up its rights, and an unyielding and upright determination; and Maurois never knew indifference or lassitude for mankind and life.

I began by evoking Maurois' immense curiosity about man; I shall conclude by stressing his infinite love of life—not life with a capital "L," but humble, modest life which is won and deserved from day to day. And I can think of no better way to conclude than by letting him address you in his own words, and thereby letting him indirectly introduce his lectures which he anticipated with delight to present to you. This passage is taken from one of his last works, *Open Letter to a Young Man:*

"Real life—look, it is all around you. It is in the flowers on your lawn, in the little lizard that basks in the sun on your balcony, in the little children who look up at their mother with tenderness, in the lovers who cling to each other, in all of these little houses where families try to hold themselves together, to love and to play. Nothing is important without these humble destinies. Their sum makes up humanity. Only men are so easily fooled. For a few undefined words they are ready to kill, to feel persecuted, to hate. Inasmuch as it is in your power to do so, call them back to the true life, to the simple pleasures and affections.

"And for yourself choose to live, and not to play a role you do not believe in, in a tragic comedy. Life is too short to be small."

Remarks by Jacques Barzun

IT IS appropriate that André Maurois' last production should be about Illusion: he was always haunted by the idea. His impulse toward the novel would naturally encourage this preoccupation, for the novel depicts the interplay between appearance and reality. And his impulse toward biography also fed this concern, for his chosen subjects were men and women of powerful imagination, often driven to creativeness by the same interplay.

Near the beginning of Maurois' career, before he had decided whether to write lives or to write fiction, he called one of his books *Mape or the World of Illusion*. That was forty years ago, but I remember my puzzled astonishment on reading the prologue to the three short tales that make up the work. "Mape" (in French *Meïpe*) is the name that a little girl gives to the country she has invented in order to escape the harsh rule of her governess.

What is startling is not this piece of child psychology, which has nothing to do with the contents of the adult stories in the book; the surprise is the curious conclusion of this prologue, in which Maurois makes two assertions. One is that the great artists create worlds of illusion which become as necessary to us as Mape was to the little girl. The other is that for every man after a certain age, happiness is to be found only in Mape.

The notion of art as illusion, which Maurois develops in the final chapter of the present book, is not new; it is indeed classical, though given fresh impetus by Freud. But it is not a satisfactory notion, since it is plain that everybody wants to dispel illusion, whereas everybody (or nearly) wants to embrace art.

Again, difficult as it may be to define art, defining illusion is harder still. For when illusion really illudes, it acquires reality; it acts like a truth and breeds results in reality. As Maurois says, art makes people think and act as if its symbols were facts of nature: Hamlet and Mickey Mouse have become part of common experience. Yet their pragmatic truth is no deception. On stage or screen, the so-called illusion illudes no one. So where is the illusion in art, and why does illusion work in desirable ways, regardless of its power to deceive?

All this is enough to make the head swim, and we must at least agree that our author has a genuine subject. But there is more: what about the illusion that is consciously used to bridge the gap between ignorance and truth, as when science throws out hypotheses, invents entities ahead of experience, or posits axioms contrary to fact? Does it not begin to seem as if we ought to revise our classification and not simply try to separate "illusion" from "reality," but rather draw distinctions among many "qualities of belief," for which in time we may coin new names?

We could then keep the word "illusion" for the simple and temporary material mistake, often ludicrous, which is the basis of comedy and of life's petty annoyances. By chance, I associate my last glimpse of Maurois with one of these, which he—philosophic as always—both grumbled at and appreciated. We were at a reception in New York; it was midwinter, and as we were leaving together it was apparent that Maurois had on an overcoat which was not his: it engulfed him like a tent; his hands were way out of sight. He saw my glance and explained that he had attended a luncheon at a hotel, where the coatroom attendant had produced this garment in place of his own. Nor was the right one among the other coats left. I said it sounded like a desperate case. "Not so desperate," replied Maurois, "because I found the owner's name on the inside pocket of this one and recognized it." He named a well-known musician. —"Then all is well?"—"Not so well as you might think, because when I called Mr. T., he said that the coat in his possession was certainly not mine: he is taller than I am—as you see from his coat which I have on—and the one he has is a good deal too big for him. So we're looking for the Third Party before we make our exchange."

I never heard the end of this coatroom farce; but before turning the page and proceeding to Maurois' discussion of his favorite theme, I leave the reader with the question, not whose overcoat was which, but what does a temporary illusion teach us about life? The origin of the error was probably a matter of tickets and numbers. But to anyone with ratiocinative powers, it is evident that the man who took Maurois' overcoat did not put it on; he walked off carrying it over his arm. And the modest exercise of reason and imagination which leads to that result confirms our hope that illusion is not the great enemy we suppose: the enemy is rather the failure of reason and imagination to assign each appearance its place in reality, its right degree of belief, so as to make it do its proper work—in science, in art, or in life.

Contents

Illusions

Illusions of the Senses and
of the Sentiments

YOUR CHOICE, this year, of a man of letters to deliver the Pegram Lectures shows your intention of associating the humanities with science. Since I believe in the fruitfulness and in the necessity of such an association, I am highly gratified by your decision. To be sure I realize that it would be rash to discuss here the sciences of which you are so much more than I the masters. In matters of physics, chemistry, biology I have acquired only a layman's rudiments. So if my theme, *illusions,* leads me to venture into those fields which are your own, I shall do so prudently and with diffidence.

I hope to be able to show you that my subject, *illusions,* is important and that it embraces all the activities of the human mind, from perception to dreams, from sentiments to intelligence, from politics to science itself. We shall have to determine the part played by illusions in the life of man, to what extent they are dangerous, and whether on the contrary they are not, in certain cases, salutary. In our opening lecture we shall examine the nature of illusions, taking as examples some of the illusions of the senses and of the sentiments; in the second lecture, the illusions of intelligence, and at that point we shall seek to define the role that science may play in dissipating, in part, these illusions; in our third and final lecture we shall study those voluntary illusions known as the fine arts, for it is obvious that when he sees a play or reads a novel the spectator or the reader seeks an illusion which he recognizes as such, in which he does not believe, but which he often finds of greater value than truth itself.

I shall immediately outline the master themes which it is my intention to develop. I believe, having meditated at length upon our subject, that man's illusions stem in major part from the fact that he projects his thoughts, his prejudices and his passions upon nature. Trees, rivers, the stars desire nothing, express nothing. It is we who invest them with our own anguish, our fears, our hopes. We then have the illusion that they cause, or even share, these emotions. We shall see that science fundamentally consists of purging phenomena of the individual errors and the human sentiments which we foist upon them. Conversely we shall find that the arts introduce into the world of facts and things the highest possible proportion of the artist's personal impressions and, more generally speaking, the highest possible proportion of humanity as a whole. Science and the arts would thus seem to be complementary. But I must not anticipate. I merely wished to give you a glimpse of the ultimate goal toward which we shall direct our steps.

I have no intention, when speaking of the illusions of the senses and of dreams, of drawing upon a complicated vocabulary, or of having recourse either to the contradictory theories of Gestalt psychology and of intellectualist philosophies, or to the symbols of Freudianism, or yet to the experiments (interesting though they may be) of the neurophysiologists. That is not my design. The examples I intend to use will be very simple, some of them familiar since men have been capable of thought, the others personal. So I ask you not to be surprised if my remarks are devoid of technical terms, controversy and polemics. What I seek to be, in these lectures, is an average human being who, in all good faith, is trying to understand. That and nothing more. I crave your patience. Along such a rocky path as this we can advance but step by step.

We are victims of illusion when we believe that we see, touch and hear things that do not exist, that we have feelings we do not actually feel, that we understand things we do not actually understand. But we must immediately establish the difference between the mistake, which we correct as soon as we recognize it as such, and the lasting illusion which persists even after we have understood its mechanism.

This morning, as I was putting on my shoes, it seemed to me that one of them was cracked from heel to toe. Surprised and concerned I leaned over and saw that what I had taken for a crack was only the shoelace. It was a different shade of black from the shoe on which it lay, thus giving this false impression. False? Well, not exactly. My eyes had not deceived me. Having realized my mistake I saw the same image as before, but I had changed my interpretation.

Another example: in my own home, in the half light of an early morning, I see, thrown over an armchair, a woman's coat with a light fur lining. So I say to myself, "Well, well! A visitor at this early hour? How very curious!" And I go through the apartment, looking for my caller; there is nobody around. I come back to the armchair and take a closer look. The coat is not a woman's coat at all; it is my own, which I had hung over the back of the chair the evening before, and on which I had left lying, lengthwise, a beige scarf. In the half light the scarf had played the part of the fur lining. Once again the data had not changed; I was merely interpreting them more accurately. The illusion fades. It was just a mistake.

In fact every perception is an interpretation, sometimes conscious, more often unconscious. The naïve concept is that nature, living beings and inanimate things alike, confronts us with objects which our senses may explore, but which we can in no way change. This is not true. Descartes leans out of his window and sees hats and coats below. He says: "I see men down there." In fact he sees neither their faces nor their bodies. His senses have supplied him with ambiguous evidence which may, *perhaps,* reveal the presence of men beneath his window.

I look at a box and say to myself: "I see a cube." Actually I cannot perceive a cube when I see only three of its sides, but I know, from long experience, that a certain pattern of the angles of intersection, of the flat surfaces in the shape of parallelograms and of the shadows are the signs of the presence of a cube. If, in turn, my sense of touch explores this cube, it will also discover the angles and the hard, smooth surfaces, but not a cube. Furthermore, how can I be sure that the thing I see is the same as what I touch? Plato himself wondered by what operation of sense we fused the perceptions derived from different senses applied to a single object, since the sense of touch does not see, and sight gives no sense of touch. The cube is not an evidence of our senses; it is a mental construct of our mind.

Gestalt psychologists refuse to distinguish between what is felt and what is deduced. "When I perceive a cube," writes Merleau-Ponty, "it is not because my reason re-thinks the apparent perspectives and, by thinking of them, re-creates the geometric definition of the cube. Far from correcting them, I do not even notice these apparent perspectives; through what I see, I am of the cube itself through its own evidence." I confess that I don't understand what "I am of the cube itself through its own evidence" means. Still we see the purpose, which is to demonstrate that perception is an older factor of the world than intelligence. Well, so be it, and that is why I used the expression mental "construct." But, as we shall see, this does nothing to change illusions. Whether it is a matter of older mental constructs or of intelligence, interpretation remains the origin of illusions.

The cube (and, for that matter, the whole of nature) comes to me in the guise of a flat surface, closely applied to my eyes, and upon which a picture has been painted. To this flat surface our experience adds perspective and relief. An excellent "trompe l'oeil" or deceptive still life painter could give me the illusion of a third dimension, thanks to a faultless imitation of all the symbols which I am used to interpret as those of objects in relief. In such a case it is only through movement that I shall be able to dissipate the illusion for, when I move, the objects so deceptively painted do not change their positions with respect to each other, as real objects in relief would.

Let me remark that our knowledge of distance and of depth is not innate. The newborn baby is unable to judge distances. You can watch him in his crib, awkwardly conducting his experiments. Our budding physicist is groping his way by use of the experimental method. As soon as he is left alone he beats the table with his rattle or his fist. He is learning to associate a sound and a direction. He tries to grasp some object hanging above him, fails, and tirelessly tries, tries again. And that is how the baby discovers the world and its simplest laws. Knowledge acquired through the senses already partakes of the nature of science, and science itself will be but a more accurate perception.

Illusion will exist in the fullest meaning of the term when no experiment, even should it convince the mind, is able to undeceive the senses. As reminders let me quote some classical instances. They may be old, but all that is old is also new. "Every thought is the newest of all things, and likewise the oldest, just like Spring," writes Alain. If you place a stick partly in and partly out of water, you will see it crooked at the water's surface. Take it out of the water and you will realize that it is straight. However, although our intelligence now knows that it is straight, it will seem crooked again if we put it back into the water. Science teaches that this is due to the refraction of light caused by the liquid medium. We understand what the scientist tells us; we believe him, but we go on seeing a crooked stick.

Another example well known to philosophers: the moon seems bigger at the horizon than at its zenith; actually it is no bigger, nor is this an effect of refraction. If, with the help of a taut string, we measure the moon at its zenith and at the horizon we shall find the same diameter. Here it is not the material medium which is involved, as in the case of the stick. The cause of the illusion is the presence of that enormous globe among the chimney pots, the houses and the trees. Our own amazement magnifies the moon. Check and re-check your measurements; they will avail you nothing. You *know* that the moon is no bigger; you will go on seeing it bigger. The surrounding objects have embodied your surprise.

A third example: a stereoscope shows us an image in relief; yet it only offers to our eyes two plane images. But these two slightly different images reproduce what our two eyes would see, were one single image to be shown in relief. We do not go through a conscious mental process, saying: "These two images are not precisely superimposed, and that is why we see an image in relief." No, experience has established within us a kind of mental structure which operates automatically and sends the message: object in relief.

A last example, familiar throughout the ages: if we cross two fingers, the forefinger and the middle finger, and place between them a marble, or the tip of our nose, we feel not one object but two. Why? Because we have brought together, in this crossed position, two surfaces which normally are not close, the left side of the forefinger and the right side of the middle finger. Once more we have not gone through the conscious mental process: "The distance between these two parts of my hand is such that they could not simultaneously feel one single small object." No. There too experience has established indestructible mental relationships. I *know*, I *see* that there is only one object. I cannot help feeling two. This phenomenon is important, for even among the activities of our intelligence, even among those of science itself, we shall run across mental structures and habits of thought that we shall find most difficult to eradicate. Francis Bacon called them "idols."

Thus, in the cases which we have studied, illusions seem to stem from this: we attribute to objects properties which derive only from our own bodies or from our mental habits. We project ourselves upon nature and, I repeat, the great task incumbent upon science will consist in expunging from reality that which stems from the observer. That we invest objects with subjective elements is obvious. A sick man will state, in perfect good faith, that all the food he is given tastes bitter, while observers consider it excellent. He is projecting his ailing condition upon his roasts, vegetables and fruit. One woman will feel too hot in a room where another may be shivering, because the former is feverish or has high blood pressure, the latter not. A thermometer may bring their minds into agreement, not their bodies.

Sometimes an image may take shape within us in the absence of any object at all. Speaking of a man who got punched in the eye, we say: "He saw stars." He did see them, because his optic nerve suffered a violent shock, which produces circumstances that correspond to a bright light appearing among surrounding objects. In this case there was no such light, but the effect of light upon his body was reproduced by the blow, and the subject projected his inner shock in the guise of "stars." The same is true of patients who suffer from the toe that has been amputated because the nerve which used to transmit messages from this toe still operates, but *in vacuo*. Electric stimuli applied to a certain region of the brain may create an image without any object.

Better still, there are cases when we see what we want to see and can at will suppress or re-create the illusion. When the train in which we are seated starts to roll, slowly and smoothly, there comes a moment at which we do not know whether it is the train at the next platform or our own which is moving. The choice is ours, and we exercise this choice by selecting (or not) an outer point of reference.

Merleau-Ponty denies this. "For if it is true," he says, "that my train and the next one may seem to me to be alternatively in motion when one of them starts, we must note that this illusion is not arbitrary, and that I cannot provoke it at will by the strictly intellectual and dispassionate choice of a point of reference. If I am playing cards in my compartment, it is the other train which will start to roll. If, on the contrary, I am looking for someone in the other train, then it will be mine which starts. On each occasion the stationary point is the one where we have our being and which is for the time our habitat. Movement and repose are apportioned to us within our surroundings, not on the basis of such hypotheses as it pleases our intelligence to elaborate but on the basis of the manner in which we situate ourselves in the world." Well, I tried the experiment; I was not playing cards; I was looking for nobody in the next train. I was totally neutral and, at will, created the illusion thanks to the choice of a point of reference. For that matter, there is a simpler example still. Psychologists have all mentioned the drawings of figures in relief in which the human will can bring forward or thrust backward one of the angles of intersection, thus modifying the image. This impression is so vivid that you believe you can see the object represented move and breathe.

I once cut a curious cartoon out of *The New Yorker*. It represented a series of diminishing rectangles, vertically arranged, their sides parallel and nested one within the other. Looking at the drawing you see it as a flat surface. Then the artist introduces a little human being into his design. In the succeeding drawings this figure grows shorter and shorter. Upon which you no longer see a two-dimensional design, but a long hotel corridor down which a man is walking. Divert your attention from the man, look at the rectangles only and you will see the flat design again. Come back to the man; once more the drawing takes on perspective and the hotel corridor reappears.

Man never perceives the images of the surrounding world without investing them with some of his own substance. Show the same picture composed of vaguely structured objects to two groups: an experimental group of really hungry people and a control group of people who have had plenty to eat. The hungry ones will identify in the drawing a far greater number of eatables.* Why? Because they invest things with their own hunger. That anthropomorphism which consists of attributing human reactions to animals or things is one of the causes of illusions. Today's younger French writers (like Robbe-Grillet) are engaged in a struggle against anthropomorphic effects. They are quite right. We speak of "capricious" weather, of a "cruel" sea, as though nature had fits of bad temper. Nature neither feels nor thinks.

The gods of old were the projections of man's desires and of his dreads. A dense, dark forest abounds in terror for primitive man. He fears who knows what, something hidden, not behind the tree, but inside it. This fear is within us; it projects our own shadow upon things. Man, who cannot bear living with this

* Fourastié.

fear, reacts upon the tree trunk or the root, carving the wood so as to fashion a god with human face, with whom he may converse. Whence the sylvans, the satyrs and the god Pan himself. At the stage of rustic religions, a god is no more than a "potential god." So the Greek mariners peopled their seas with Sirens, Nereids and Tritons.

The gods of Olympus, Homer's gods, are projections upon the outer world of the subject's own affective states. "Ajax says that he is pressed onward by a god; it is because he feels his hands and feet moving with a will of their own. And if, on the contrary, Jupiter should this day send victory to the Trojans, this means that the Achaean knees have come to a halt." If Helen seeks to justify her acts by declaring that Venus has possessed her, it means that, at a crucial moment, her desire was stronger than her will. "These metaphors are all accurate; the phrase rings true; supernaturally the scene is what it would be physiologically." * Homer's heroes believe in the gods of Olympus; they recognize in them and in nature forces of good and evil which are beyond them. What a temptation it must have been to attribute the mysterious thunderclap to the wrath of Jupiter, and the miraculous rainbow to a messenger of the gods! Science, by explaining thunder and rainbow, will strip Olympus of its gods.

May I revert to the idea, essential to our subject, that we elaborate explanations by the use, conscious or not, of our prior experience and of the mental structures formed by this experience? At times our fears and our beliefs are the sole reality, and we imagine all the rest. May I cite a personal example? In France,

* Alain.

on the sixth of January or "Twelfth Night" (Jour des Rois), we share a cake (la Galette des Rois), into the dough of which the cook has slipped a dry bean or a tiny human figure. The guest who finds the bean in his slice becomes the King. One year, while eating my slice I cried out: "I've swallowed the bean." "Oh, that's too bad," said my wife, "it was a china bean." That night I felt severe pains in my stomach. The bean was giving trouble. The next morning, my pain growing worse, I said to my son: "I must go to the doctor's and have an X-ray taken; I swallowed the bean." He answered: "That's impossible; we finished the cake after you left and it was I who got the bean." He was right; I had not swallowed anything at all; possibly a fragment of crust, harder than the rest, had produced this illusion. It had made me feel sicker than the actual bean would have done.

We see what we think we see. The Russian screen director Poudovkine one day shot a dead pan close-up of the actor Mosjoukine. He screened this take so as to follow, first a plate of soup, next a young woman lying dead in her coffin, and last a child playing with a teddy bear. The audience noticed that Mosjoukine cast a pensive eye on the soup, a sorrowful gaze on the corpse, and that he looked at the child with a radiant smile. But in fact the same shot of an expressionless Mosjoukine had been used all three times. * The same experiment was tried with the Japanese actor Sessue Hayakawa. His face, absolutely impassive, reflected all the passions of the audience. Their minds had acted out the tragedy, and their minds alone.

Just as preconceived ideas can make us see what does not exist, so they can stop us from seeing or hearing what does. A

* Merleau-Ponty.

French scholar, M. Fourastié, gives a curious example of this. He had an American friend who lived in France in a small suburb of Paris called Garches. This American, who spoke very fluent French, one day said to Fourastié: "It's curious. I can make myself understood all over France without the slightest difficulty, but when I tell a taxidriver to take me to Gâches, he can't understand." You will have noticed that this American pronounced it "Gâches," without rolling the "R". "So," he went on, "I write the word down on a bit of paper, show it to the driver, who reads it and says: 'Ah! Gâches,' and takes me straight home. Can you explain this mystery?" The American did *not* hear the taxidriver pronouncing the word "Garches," because he was expecting "Gâches." Unconsciously he had erased the "R". This type of illusion explains the failure of many an international conference, for it is not only individual letters but ideas too that we fail to hear, that we erase because they are not included in our personal catalogue. In France, when talking of political discussions, we often speak of a "debate between two deaf men." The expression is apt. There is none so deaf as he who will not hear. An argument which might throw us off balance because it weakens our position, slides off us unnoticed.

In short, every single perception depends upon the nature of him who perceives, upon his experience and his memories. It is this fragment of himself, which he introduces among things, that makes illusions possible. In the case of daydreams, the subject supplies almost everything. For instance, in the sound of a train he will hear a Beethoven symphony. Of course there is no such symphony. If he listens more carefully all he can hear is the rhythmic rumble of the wheels on the track, but the sound served as a prop for his daydream. The traveler hummed the symphony under his breath and his muted voice served as a further prop. He is even able to superimpose binary and tertiary rhythms upon the noise of the train. The clouds in their splendor, the dancing flames of a wood fire, the movement of the leaves in a dusky grove provide the evanescent and mobile backdrop before which the dreamer may, at will, conjure up the traits which will reveal a face dear to him, a monster, or the wild ride of the Valkyries. Here it is not a total illusion, for we do not believe that our daydreams correspond to any actual existence. We can withdraw from them at will. But we do find illusions at their fullest strength when we dream while we sleep.

All men dream, and so do animals. All men have always had dreams, the savages and the civilized alike. And all of them have, at all times, been astonished by this secondary state of being, which bears no intelligible relationship to what we call real existence. Where did these images, with no apparent foundation, spring from? Were they sent by the gods? Did they foretell happy or unhappy events? Are they the means of release from our frustrated desires and our unavowed secrets? Efforts have always been made to detect some relationship between the fate of the dreamer and the nature of his dreams. Joseph interpreted the dreams of Pharaoh. For centuries peddlers have been selling "The Key to Your Dreams." Today psychoanalysts compile whole catalogues of symbols. Many thinkers, and by no means the least of them, Pascal for instance and Leibnitz, have asserted that reality is nothing other than closely linked dreams; others have claimed that no criteria exist which allow us to know whether, at any given moment, we are dreaming or are awake.

Let us approach the problem starting from our experience of perception. We have seen that upon a basis of sensations provoked by exterior phenomena (or on occasion by organic phenomena) we elaborate interpretations which, taken as a whole, constitute what we call reality. In our dreams images are elaborated, or so it would seem, without the support of sensations, since our eyes are closed and our body is at rest. But it has long been proved that this is but an appearance. Actually dreams do derive support from sensations. It is true that, during sleep, our eyes are closed, but the pressure of the lids excites the optic nerves and the sleeper sees phosphenes. First there will be a black background, followed by spots of different colors, some reddish, others white, and lines too, now lusterless and now "of a singular brilliance. These colored spots with their mobile shapes delineate the objects of which our dream will be made up." * This is so true that I have, on the basis of this observation, devised a method for getting to sleep. I focus my attention upon the phosphenes. I try to interpret them, just as you identify an image in an ink spot. And at the very moment when this image becomes clearer and relates to a memory, I fall asleep.

Other sources of light can become the midnight support of dreams: moonbeams, a flicker of light through a window, a turned-on lamp. Place a flame before the closed lids of a sleeper; he will dream that he is an onlooker at a fire. When water was dripped on to Maury's forehead, he dreamed that he was in Italy, all of a sweat. An American philosopher, G. T. Ledd, was once able, as he woke, to seize upon his fading dream. He then saw the objects of his dream merge with the phosphene spots. He was reading a newspaper; that was the dream. He wakes

* Alfred Maury.

up and, of the newspaper, there remain before his eyes a white spot and some vague black stripes; that is reality. Our other senses may also supply such support. Our ears bring us buzzing and whistling sounds. Some mumble in their sleep and their dream feeds on their own voice. Doors creak, the sound of footsteps comes down from the floor above, a clock strikes. The sense of touch plays an important part: the friction of the bed clothes against the body, the action of the body itself. "Sometimes," writes Marcel Proust, "just as Eve took birth from one of Adam's ribs, a woman would take birth during my sleep because of the twisted position of one of my thighs. She was a creation of the pleasure which I was about to enjoy, but I imagined that it was she who was bringing me this pleasure. My body, feeling in hers its own warmth, was striving to find itself in her. Then I would wake up." This is the nature of erotic dreams, so frequent in youth, in which the imaginary woman often takes the face of a woman the dreamer has known and coveted; for memories link up with sensations. We fashion our dreams out of both actual sensations and memories.

Greater still is the part played in dreams by intestinal sensations. Indigestion or a slight flutter of the heart gives birth to deep anguish. It has been said that anguish is fear without an object. "I'm frightened," says the patient, "but I don't know what I'm afraid of." In our dreams this objectless fear seeks its object. To explain his distress, the sleeper elaborates an interpretation based on motives for distress with which he is familiar. I often dream that I have come to a town where I am to give a lecture. On the walls I notice posters with my portrait and I read the title: *The Second Law of Thermodynamics.* Now that is a subject about which I know virtually nothing. I have no notes. I go into the auditorium; they lead me to the podium. The hall is full. Without the slightest idea of what to say I stare at the public and keep my mouth closed. Realizing that I am ridiculous, I find myself in an intolerable position, with no solution in view. This is so painful a feeling that I wake with a start. Praised be the Lord, I am in my own bed; I have no lecture to deliver; it was only a dream.

Here is another distressing dream, captured upon awaking. I am in my study. An actress by the name of Marie Saguenay has come to ask me for a play that I was to write for her. I know that I have written the play. I look for the manuscript among my papers; I cannot find it. Then I remember that my wife tidied up my papers because of a party. The manuscript has certainly got lost. Marie Saguenay starts to shout and scream: "I've rented a theatre to produce that play." I am of course extremely upset. Then I wake up, my heart beating wildly. I turn on the light and the phantoms vanish. It's really ridiculous! But I can identify the source of this interpretation of my distress. Before going to sleep I had read a history of Canada, and the name *Saguenay* had attracted my attention. It is also true that my papers had been tidied up, quite against my will, that I was finding it difficult to make head or tail of them, and that this incident had annoyed me not a little. I had been using these memories to interpret a slight touch of tachycardia.

The French humorist Tristan Bernard tells of having seen his parents in a dream, long after their death. He had loved them dearly, but in this dream he got into a violent quarrel with them over his career, of which they disapproved. Painful, in fact the very harshest, words were exchanged. The scene was turning into a real scandal, quite unbearable. This excellent son is harrowed by remorse. The violence of his emotion awakens him. He gathers his wits together. The entire melodramatic scene is utterly fantastic since he no longer has parents. "But, of course, they are dead," he says to himself, "how very fortunate!"

Thus, on the basis of elementary sensations, a certain form of invention continues, during sleep, to develop fictions which are almost always both incoherent and absurd. The dreams of which we tell often seem to have a fairly rational structure, but the narrator is then awake. He brings order out of chaos. "Who can remember a dream as it was dreamt? We call dream what is already the interpretation of a dream." Jung, in his autobiography, describes peculiarly precise and coherent dreams. It seems very probable that, in perfectly good faith, he touched them up and completed them. Almost all retold dreams are fictionalized. "Dream thoughts do not easily lend themselves to narration. The relation of real events is consecutive, whereas dream thoughts may present a polyphonic simultaneousness which is difficult to translate into words." * Actually the instability of the images is one of the characteristics of dreams. Phosphenes evolve, a noise stops, a leg twitches and the dreamer invents episodes to explain these changes. I believe that this is one of the answers to oppose to those (like Pascal) who claim that it is impossible to distinguish between dreams and reality. In real life I can pin down an image as long as I stay in one place. Before me are a window, a picture, a pile of books. If I close my eyes ten minutes and then open them again, I still see the window,

* Delay and Pichot: "Abrégé de Psychologie."

the picture and the pile of books. The dreamer cannot pin down his dream. You may say that he does not know this. No, but when awake a man can check the permanence of his images. "Anyone can make believe that the book he is reading is a dream book," says Sartre, "but he will immediately realise, beyond all doubt, that this fiction is absurd." For in no dream would it be possible to turn the pages and to find, page after page, the orderly development of a story or of a mental process.

Pascal's objection, however, remains a strong one. If perceptions are interpretations reached with the help of memories, and if dreams too invoke memories in order to explain sensations from without (or from within), what is the difference between perceptions and dreams? We have already given one answer: stability. Here is another. We have countless memories. We have recorded and kept all the images, sounds and sensations perceived in the course of our life, just as a computer stows away in its memory all the information fed to it. You might ask: "How can this be possible? Billions of billions of images in one tiny brain?" There is virtually no limit to miniaturization. The physicist Feynman once told me that the entire text of the Bible could be reproduced on the point of a needle. It is a fact that, from time to time, from the depths of our memory, up will come a face, a word, a tune which we believed we had forgotten forty years ago. It would seem that nothing at all is ever lost, even though this fraction of our past, present within us at this moment, is so infinitesimal. We have available for our interpretations an almost unlimited store of memories; to these Jung adds those of all mankind.

The essential difference is that, while we are awake, the choice of images is very restricted by the need for action, and hence the obligation to sort out the useful images, whereas, during our sleep, this choice is untrammeled. At this precise moment, the wakeful man you see before you, engaged in delivering a lecture, allows out of his store of memories only those images and those words necessary to carry out his undertaking. Were he to admit to his consciousness other ideas, such as the charm of a lady in the audience, some memory of France, he could never finish his sentence and would stop short. If a general, in the heat of battle, were to stop thinking of strategy in order to admire the landscape, to compare it with others and to recall the poets, that battle would be lost. Action does not allow for daydreams.

Quite on the contrary, the sleeper is indifferent to the present moment, to the current state of the world and even to his own. This "non-involvement" is what characterizes sleep. Left, more or less, with its reins on its neck, memory supplies, as factors of interpretation, a gallimaufry of echoes from the past, fragments of yesterday's impressions, and remnants from times gone by, long buried beneath the years. Naturally this collection of random factors produces an incoherent tale which imagination then strives to correct with the help of other memories. The result is no more intelligible, and further strata have to be explored. That is why, in dreams, so many things happen so fast. The sleeper has the illusion of having slept for ten years. He has actually been dreaming for ten minutes.

Maury's dream about the Reign of Terror is a well-known case. He witnesses the massacres, appears before the Revolutionary Tribunal, sees Robespierre, Marat, Fouquier-Tinville. He is judged, condemned to death, carted off to the guillotine in a

tumbrel, made fast to the grisly board. The blade comes down
on his neck. He wakes in a state of acute distress and discovers
that the head of his bedstead, which had worked loose, had
fallen onto his cervical vertebrae. In a few seconds this external
sensation had given body to a dream where all these events had
successively occurred. Maury's dream and the conclusion he
drew from it have been disputed and, actually, we may well
wonder whether, in his dream, the story was as substantial as it
turned out to be in his memory of that same dream, during
which the events were probably foreshortened. When he awoke
his conscious intelligence filled in the gaps. As a matter of fact
our memory soon sweeps away the scattered remnants of our
dreams. These raw materials are of no help to action. Conse-
quently almost all of them are forgotten. And yet our memory
occasionally puts by fragments of dreams which go on worrying
us. Was it really a dream? Was I awake? I no longer can tell.

A French writer, Roger Caillois, is the author of an essay,
"The Uncertainty Which Stems from Dreams," in which he in
a certain measure underwrites Pascal's doubts. He tells of having run into Denis de Rougemont at Strasburg. Rougemont had
just seen their common friend, the writer Nabokov, in Paris,
straight off the plane from London, in which he (Nabokov)
had traveled next to an unknown Chinese fast asleep in his seat.
Waking with a start this Chinese had asked Nabokov, in English: "Do you sell hardware?" and, upon receiving a negative
answer, had gone back to sleep. Nabokov's hypothesis was that
the Chinese was only half awake and still dreaming. But a few
days later it occurred to Caillois that it was perhaps not the
Chinese who had been asleep and dreaming, but rather Nabo-

kov himself who had dropped off and dreamt that the Chinese asked him whether he sold hardware. But could one not just as well imagine that Rougemont had dreamt the whole story, and that Nabokov hadn't told him anything at all? "Then, in turn," adds Caillois, "I had no proof that Rougemont really told me this tale; I might have dreamt it myself. Then I glimpsed the later possibility of every reader of these pages wondering whether he had actually read them, or whether he had not more probably dreamt this dialectic, at once rigorously logical and demented, as is the nature of the dialectics of dreams. To be sure any such chain reaction of hypotheses is highly theoretical. It would be difficult to check them. Nabokov might have forgotten the incident. As to the Chinese, even if he were found, how could one reasonably expect that he would remember having, years before and while half asleep, put such an incongruous question to a fellow traveler on board a plane? We are definitely brought to admit that memory is not always able to distinguish between the recollection of a dream and that of reality."

The difficulty in this strange case seems a major one because it is a matter of narratives and of narratives re-narrated. But Caillois sees this uncertainty as extending to all instances and holds that it is always impossible to know whether we are dreaming, or whether we dream that we are dreaming, or dream that we are awake. He quotes a famous fable of the Taoist philosopher Tchoang-tsen: "One night, long ago, I was a butterfly, satisfied with its fluttering fate. Then I awoke as Tchoang-tsen. But am I a philosopher who remembers having dreamt that he was a butterfly, or am I a butterfly who now dreams that it is the philosopher Tchoang-tsen?" We have already mentioned Pascal's opinions. "Were we to dream the same thing every night," says Pascal, "it would affect us just as much as the objects we see every day." Yes, but we do not dream the same thing every night. Because our dreams differ, what we see in them affects us far less than what we see when awake, just because of that lack of continuity. When in real life there occurs a break in that continuity, for instance when we travel fast, constantly changing scenes and environment, we may well say: "I must be dreaming," for our life has turned into a dream, a slightly more consistent dream.

But this state is a rare one. Life is not made of the stuff of dreams. It is dreams that are made of the stuff of life. If this audience were suddenly, as in a motion picture fade-out, to change into an aviary full of birds, I should be dreaming. I should not be aware of it, but the surprise might well awaken me. Then I should realize that the aviary was an illusion, that birds cannot possibly come to listen to a lecture, that my presence here is in line with my whole life history and, in short, that "continuity allows us to conclude that this world is the real world." The illusion persists unconquered as long as we are asleep; it cannot survive our awakening.

A noteworthy point is that a dreamer is often happy to wake up in order to escape from a bad dream, whereas the wakeful man, on the contrary, baptizes "dream" an imaginary creation designed to gratify a desire or to dismiss some harsh reality. "What a lovely dream," say the unfortunate, trying to picture happiness. So we have the wakeful man eager for dreams and the sleeper generally anxious to wake up. Perhaps this is because dreams are ambivalent, now terrifying and now delightful. It has been observed that an infant, deprived of its bottle at the usual time, will have a dream in the course of which the movements of its lips reveal that it is sucking at an imaginary bottle, and it will smile happily, even though only two or three days old, whereas it does not smile while awake before the age of two or three months. There is nothing surprising about such precocious dreams. As soon as psychic life exists so, necessarily, do dreams. Proust writes: "If I have always been so deeply interested in dreams, . . . , is it not because, compensating for their evanescence by their intensity, they help you better to understand, for instance, the subjectivity of love?" For dreams can, in a few minutes, make us fall passionately in love with an ugly woman, "just as if, invented by some miraculous physician, they were intravenous injections of love." The amorous suggestion fades away with equal speed, our midnight beloved turns ugly again, "but something more precious still also fades away, a whole delightful fresco of tender feelings, of sensual joys, of vague, hazy regrets . . . which we should have liked to keep for our waking hours, but which vanishes like some dimming patch of color, too pale for us to recapture it."

Yes, there are sweet dreams which correspond to a state of bodily well-being, to the absence of any obstacle, but upon our awakening they fade away as fast as do nightmares. Neither is known to us otherwise than through a memory which is, of necessity, a composition. We restructure and redesign our dreams to put them into form and that is why I deeply mistrust the ingenious interpretations which can be found for them. Some hold that our shameful desires, repressed in our waking hours, stand revealed in our dreams. "I don't know if it is because I am lacking in modesty," writes Caillois, "but I have never seen anything in a dream that I should be unwilling to recognize when awake." Others believe that our sleep is haunted by archetypal patterns, dredged up from our millennial past; thus Jung in his dreams would read the texts of the alchemists of the Middle Ages or of the sixteenth century. But desires and archetypal patterns alike come to us in the shape of symbols and we fall back upon interpretation, that is to say, often enough, upon illusion. Alain was mistrustful of what he called supine philosophy, and of the closed-lidded thinker. "A dream means that I have ill perceived that which exists. Yes, people say, but it is quite possible that this kind of mistake may reveal to me my deep self and my true thoughts. Is this not an admirable conceit, that my true thoughts should be mistaken ones?"

Marcel Proust used to maintain that one could imagine, after death, the spirit's surviving the body, and going on thinking thoughts, without the support of sensations, these now inconceivable since the organs of the senses had ceased to function. This disembodied life would be of the nature of a dream and would be made up of the incongruous procession, now delightful, now terrifying, of all the millions of images which form our past. Man would awake from the dream of life only to pass into an eternal dream from which he could never awaken. All that seems to me most unlikely, for a dead organism no longer supplies support in the form of sensations.

Hallucination is somewhat different from illusion. In an illusion the error stems from the interpretation. In an hallucination it is the sensation itself which is garbled. Aldous Huxley tried to analyze the mechanics of this phenomenon by inducing it with hallucinogenic drugs. He described his impressions after ingesting mescaline. The world about him stood transfigured. The books on his shelves were glittering and bright. A bunch of flowers seemed to have assumed a deep meaning. A chair revealed supernatural beauty such that the sight of a chair painted by Van Gogh seemed but an empty symbol. What he, Huxley, saw was the Being, the secret essence of all things, as the mystics see it. His perception of colors was unbelievably enhanced. In the drabbest stuffs he discovered crimson, blue and green draperies worthy of the great Italian painters. "This is how we should always be able to see," he said to himself.

Why does mescaline give this feeling of superhuman beauty and fulfilment? Aldous Huxley adopts a suggestion of Bergson's. The function of the brain and of the nervous system is to eliminate, not to produce. Every human being would seem at any time potentially capable of remembering everything that had ever happened to him, and of perceiving everything that occurs in the universe. (Remember how it has proved possible to establish contact with a spatial device thousands of miles away. It is conceivable that the slightest occurrence at Pekin or Melbourne may produce here at Brookhaven minute effects that could be recorded by some ultrasensitive apparatus.) Yes, but a man would be engulfed by this tide of information if its billows were to break over him. Most of it would be of no use to him. The role of the brain and of the organs of sense, according to Bergson and Huxley, is to sort out and to give right of way only to what is of practical use for our biological survival.

All the rest is eliminated; but if, under exceptional circumstances, such as mystical faith or drugs, the floodgates are even partly opened, then a torrent of strong impressions will pour through. That is what occurs after mescaline has been ingested. The function of the brain is coordinated by a system of enzymes. Some of these regulate the provision of glucose for the brain cells. Mescaline prevents the production of these enzymes and so deprives of glucose an organ which stands in constant need of it. Then what happens? The brain no longer functions normally. The will to act is notably decreased, while visual impressions become more varied and more vivid. The eyes recover both the innocence and the sharpness of childhood. All kinds of biologically useless sensations are liberated. The world acquires supernatural beauty, not because it has changed but because we project upon it our brain's lack of glucose. In so doing we remain in the realm of illusion and draw near to that of madness.

Hallucination can also be provoked by the stimulation of this or that zone of the brain. A woman patient whose skull has been laid open for an operation *knows* that she hears a tune. She even hums it. After the operation the surgeon discusses the phenomenon with his patient. "Oh, I know how that happened," she says, "you had a phonograph in the room." She believes this. It is a classical case of illusion. When excited, a certain zone of her brain reacted as it would have reacted to a sound, and this state was projected in the guise of a familiar tune. A disease producing the same stimulus at the same point could result in the patient's hearing voices.* The novelist Virginia Woolf, a victim of attacks of mental confusion, used to hear the birds in her garden speaking to her in Greek.

* Penfield and Jasper (Little, Brown).

A man who dreams while wide awake, and believes in his dream, is a madman. But who is not mad, more or less? As you know, the Académie Française has for more than three centuries been compiling and recompiling its dictionary. Each word is defined and examples, illustrating its use, are added. After the word *completely* someone proposed as an example: "He is completely mad." One of our members is a great psychiatrist, Dr. Delay. He protested: "Nobody is completely mad." He was right and he could have added: "Nobody is completely sane." The madman escapes from the world as other men see it and provides himself with a reassuring illusion. He takes himself for Napoleon, Mohammed or Jesus Christ because by so doing he avoids the distressing realization that he is nothing but a poor little fellow. But between the so-called sensible woman who escapes thanks to a diet of novels and the lunatic who takes herself for Queen Elizabeth, though she is actually a charwoman from Brooklyn, there is a difference of degree, not of nature. We are all of us crazier and crazier in a crazier and crazier world.

A man too delicate of spirit for the station in life into which he happens to be born is, at the outset, merely jealous and unhappy. Impelled by these feelings he elaborates an irrational image and violent criticism of society to explain away his own secret mortification. When the feelings of discontent which he tries to express are those of a whole class, or of a whole nation, the impassioned theorist becomes a prophet or a hero, whereas if he does no more than identify with a known hero, and takes himself for Lincoln or Washington, he gets thrown into a padded cell.

Jean Cocteau wrote: "Victor Hugo was a madman who took

himself for Victor Hugo." The words are apt and most profound. Victor Hugo came of a family with a history of hereditary insanity. He himself heard voices, had visions. But as he also possessed an incomparable genius for words, he turned his hallucinations into masterpieces. Having achieved glory he had a perfect right to proclaim: "I am a prophet." The world accepts the folly of the poet because the poet transmutes his frenzy into marvelous language. Similarly we could say: "Napoleon was a madman who took himself for Napoleon." He had formed a certain image of himself and for fifteen years enforced this illusion upon Europe. But he had kept close enough contact with reality to enable him, after his fall, to adapt himself to a new and distressing reality without losing his head.

It is almost every man's fate to act out a part, but most of them are able, when it becomes necessary, to cast aside their mask and to see themselves as others see them. We are all, as Pirandello had it, characters in search of an author. Of an author who is none other than ourself. The wisest suit their part to their voice and their temperament, thanks to which they are able to remain natural. But rare indeed are those who never have any illusions. How many women there are who believe themselves beloved by a man who is scarcely conscious of them. In the tritest expressions, in strictly conventional greetings, in a look, they will discover signs which they then interpret. Conversely we may have the illusion of being no longer loved, when actually no threat to our love exists. "What can the matter be?" wonders the man in love. "She's not her usual self. She seems embarrassed, moody. She doesn't love me any more." She seemed embarrassed because she had a run in her stocking or because her shoe pinched. A mistake in interpretation, an illusion.

I have mentioned the Académie Française. As you know, that body has forty members. When a vacancy occurs candidates declare themselves and pay calls upon the academicians. How many times have I not had a candidate tell me, after going the rounds: "I found the warmest of welcomes; I can count on twenty sure votes." But I, having spoken freely with his electors, give him four at the outside. When the ballots are counted he gets two. What has happened? He had interpreted signs. "X told me he'd be happy to see me join the Académie. [Perhaps he'd be happy, but he'll do nothing to help you get in.] X saw me right out to his doorstep. [He is a courteous gentleman, and all the more so since he did not intend to give you his vote.]" A mistake in interpretation, an illusion; brief encounter with folly.

Leaving the realm of the senses for that of the sentiments, we once more find the phenomenon of illusions, that is to say, the projection of our own states of mind upon living beings or events. A man in love no longer sees that woman as other women, or as heart-free men, see her. He bedecks her with his own desires. Bernard Shaw's Don Juan believes that the beloved is a creature of coral and ivory, emancipated from the enslavement of all bodily needs. Byron refused to watch a woman eat. Ian Fleming could not bear women to be sick. It wrecked his illusion. Proust very successfully shows that to the adoring Saint-Loup, Rachel appears an admirable creature, of unparalleled beauty, culture and delicacy of soul, while for the Narrator, who had known her as a venal woman, who could be enjoyed for twenty francs, Rachel is nothing at all. In the eyes of Baron Charlus, who loves men, Jupien the janitor seems desirable; in the eyes of all others, Jupien remains a third-rate, vulgar fellow.

We believe that our love is the offspring of some extraordinary encounter; actually it was born because that woman came into our life at a time when we were in love, but did not know with whom. In Proust's novel we see Odette, Gilberte, Albertine, successively illuminated by the spotlights of varying ages and sentiments, and taking on their colors, like dancers whose dress is white but under the light appears in turn yellow, green or blue. Our infatuated ego cannot even imagine what our ego will be when heart free; our young ego laughs at old man's passions, but these same passions will be ours when the spotlight of old age catches us in its beam.

For Proust the real world does not exist. We are constantly creating a world as we color it with our passions. A man in love will treasure wondrous memories of a country or of a show which he visited or shared with his beloved one. Illusion! The country was ugly and the show hackneyed, but the impassioned being is like a man wearing blue-lensed glasses who swears in good faith that the world is blue. In Tolstoy's novel, *Anna Karenina,* Levine, who has just become engaged, feels drenched with joy. For the first time he notices the beauty of houses, of trees; he has the feeling that the janitors at their doorsteps, the policemen, the cab drivers all seem kind and happy. It is not the town that has changed; it is not the drivers who have become kind; it is Levine projecting his own happiness onto all his surroundings. There is not one universe, says Proust, there are millions of them, "almost as many as there are human eyes and intellects awaking every morning."

But the very mention of illusions means that we thereby recognize the existence of a non-illusive reality and the possibility of embracing it. Otherwise how should we know that we are subject to illusions? Why did we say that seeing a bigger moon on the horizon is an illusion? Because we measured it and introduced an objective judgment. Proust knows that beyond our impressions there is an outside world common to all men which must be understood. He applies his prodigious intelligence to the analysis of all the illusions of the senses, of the sentiments and of reason.

But if he analyzes and exposes the illusions of love, it would be a mistake to believe that he seeks to dissuade men from indulging in them. Such illusions enrich our lives. We can actually observe that a man, a woman, lifted out of themselves by a great love, are worth infinitely more, despite their disappointments, than those who have never loved at all. When she reawakens in Swann the emotions which had been his as an adolescent, Odette recreated him as a more sensitive human being. Moonlight, the beauty of all things move him as they used to in the days of his youth. Sensual love may be transformed into a love of the arts, into a poem, or into heroism. It leads us not only to the greatest sacrifices for the sake of the loved one, but at times even to the sacrifice of our love itself. Proust realized the value of the illusion whose vigor is such that it uproots from our hearts the tares of habit, skepticism, levity and indifference.

To be sure love is not the only sentiment that distorts reality.

All passions show us the projection of our own desire rather than the object itself. Hate like love begets illusions. Of a man we hate we are ready to believe anything, applying no critical judgment. Then there are collective illusions. A political party will scorn or denigrate anything done by its rival, while adoring or lauding all that comes from its chief. For a pro-Chinese the *Thoughts of Mao* is a breviary of quasi-divine wisdom; for a layman it is a tissue of second-rate platitudes. During wars the two sides mutually accuse each other of committing atrocities. Each of them is blind to those he commits himself. Just as, to understand the phenomenon of the crooked stick in the water, we must correct it by intelligent analysis, so must a philosopher or a wise man seek to correct his sentiments. A philosopher in love will, in so far as his love is concerned, be as mad as the mere man in the street. "None can ensure that a man shall have no passions." But he may endeavor to reach a high degree of objectivity which will enable him to divest real facts of the errors projected upon them by his passion.

This will be an arduous task. The object of this first lecture was to remind us that most men, for different reasons, do not see the world as it is, and this is dangerous, for how shall they determine their conduct, how organize this world if they have but a distorted image of it? The purpose of science will be to correct this image. We shall see, in the second lecture, how science seeks to attain this end and to what extent its efforts are successful.

The Illusions of Science

WE NOW REACH matters more closely connected with the objects of your daily research. Does science rid man of his illusions? Is science itself an illusion? Can illusions survive in a scientific and technological age? As I have said I shall advance prudently along this path, and not without fear. But you would have it so; I can but comply. You will forgive the layman's mistakes.

A French Nobel Prize winner for literature, Saint-John Perse, once told me that one day, while he was living in Washington, Einstein called him up from Princeton and asked him to come and see him. "I have a question to ask you," said Einstein. Saint-John Perse naturally complied and this was the question: "How does a poet work? How does the idea of a poem come to him? How does this idea grow?" Saint-John Perse described the vast part played by intuition and by the subconscious. Einstein seemed delighted: "But it's the same thing for the man of science," he said. "The mechanics of discovery are neither logical nor intellectual. It is a sudden illumination, almost a rapture. Later, to be sure, intelligence analyzes and experiments confirm (or invalidate) the intuition. But initially there is a great forward leap of the imagination."

We shall come back later to the bonds between the man of

science and the poet. However, it is important to observe at the outset that science, contrary to art, is above all a method of eliminating illusions. No doubt, as Einstein said, discovery blossoms forth from an intuition which, in turn, perhaps stems from an unconscious statistical recollection or from the sudden glimpse of an analogy. But the scientist consciously draws working hypotheses from these intuitions, after which he submits both intuitions and hypotheses to the test of experiment. He strives to do this not only by means of his senses but with ever more highly perfected instruments. His role is in the greatest measure possible to divest things of the illusions which partake of the nature of the observer and of his preconceived ideas. One physician states: "This patient has anemia." Another does not think so. Blood count and analysis will, for this particular point, establish the scientific truth, acceptable to any human mind. One observer remarks: "The explosions of those two stars were simultaneous." Another rejoins: "No, they were separated by an interval of time." Einstein answers: "You were not in the same spot. Take into account your respective positions and the speed of light, and you will find yourself in agreement." In short the scientific observer embraces, ever more closely, a truth which he strives to make objective, that is to say, independent of himself and of his reasoning. "The world is no matter for guess-work." * It is what it is. The scientist may try to guess at it, and sometimes not unsuccessfully. Le Verrier guessed the existence of a planet, and exist it did. Monod and Jacob guessed at an untried acid, acting as a messenger, and later discovered it. But had nature's answer been negative they would have accepted it without any hesitation.

* Berthelot.

So far so good, but this outline of science calls for a *first reservation*: The technical quality of observation is linked to the scope of our instruments. Before Copernicus, to rational men the earth seemed to be the center of the universe; the invention of the telescope was to destroy this illusion. Before the microscope men knew nothing of microbes; they could not fail to have illusions regarding the nature of infectious diseases. With electron microscopes they can observe not only bacteria but viruses as well. Tomorrow perhaps some even more highly perfected microscopes will allow us to penetrate even more deeply into the world of the infinitely small. Experiments carried out at a given time, with given sets of instruments, at a given level of dimensions, suggest an image of the world which is the best possible at that level. But it would be an illusion to believe that the science of this level is definitive. Science marches on, through error after error, along the road to the "perfect" knowledge, which it will never reach, of a "reality" with which we have no direct contact.

A second reservation: Even with instruments which he has striven to make as perfect as possible, man in the last analysis only perceives the data supplied by the instruments through his own senses. Behind the lenses of the telescope or the microscope there is a human eye. Replace this eye by some more powerful artificial eye. There will still be a man using and interpreting the results registered by the artificial eye, as indeed by any other device. Now the equipment of our senses and of our intelligence, satisfactory as it is for our daily existence (and for that matter shaped to *serve* that existence over a long evolutionary period), is not so constituted as to be able to embrace the whole of reality. We have but two eyes, two ears, two hands; we are

sensitive to a small number of radiations only. We can imagine
beings endowed with more senses than we, and with more
highly refined organs. Their knowledge of the world would be
more complete than ours. And these beings could in turn
imagine others, still better equipped by nature, and freer still
from illusions. With each higher degree of perfection the concept of the world would be transformed, but no final boundary
would ever be reached. Science presents, and will ever present,
not the faithful image of an objective reality that exists, albeit
beyond our reach, but rather the image of the relationship between man and an unknown reality.

The physicist seeks to determine whether something is true or
false. True or false for whom? Of course he does not claim, as
did that astounding bishop, George Berkeley, that everything
takes place within his own mind. Absolute idealism is certainly
an illusion. Otherwise how could a number of observers ever
reach agreement on the phenomena of the outer world? To explain such agreement we should have to invoke Leibnitz's
monads, and pre-established harmony. Again an illusion. There-
fore something, outside ourselves, does exist. But this eternally
inaccessible world reaches us only through our own instruments
of understanding. Plato's cave is an apt image. We are fettered
captives, with our backs to the light, and we can see only the
wall along which shadows glide past. We spend our time ob-
serving these shadows and if one of us succeeds in discovering
the laws governing their appearance and in predicting their
movements we call him a man of science, and send him to a
choice cranny of the cave called Brookhaven, and shower him
with honors. But he stays a captive for all that. When he says

"the thing" (*the thing* he is seeking) he does not mean an absolute reality which, for a human mind, remains inconceivable, but simply an appearance capable of being repeated in the course of a series of experiments.

Third reservation: However precise, however objective observation may be, illusion recurs as soon as interpretation steps in. We have remarked, when speaking of the illusions of the senses, that mistaken interpretations often have the following origin: the customary structures of our minds are superimposed upon facts for which these structures are not suited. It is impossible wholly to safeguard one's self against such mistakes. The inertia of living beings is difficult to overcome. Animals, men—even men of science—find it hard to give up their mental habits. In the swampy ground where it makes its home the Labrador duck gets its food by bearing down on the mud with its broad, webbed feet; this pressure forces up the worms to which the duck is so partial. If the same breed is reared in a zoo, on a cement floor, and is fed by its keeper, it none the less, when hungry, continues to bear down on this ungrateful surface. What has proved rewarding for so many generations of ducks cannot fail to be rewarding still.

Rational man behaves exactly like the Labrador duck. He believes that if he does what he has always done, if he reasons as his ancestors reasoned, all will be well. This, when both circumstances and human knowledge have changed, is a total illusion. Oppenheimer says that common sense is wrong if it expects what is familiar to turn up again in what is not. In the days when men thought the world was flat, the navigator, a man of common sense, sailing from Europe toward the mysterious

shores of a new world would say: "You'd have to be mad to believe the world is round; I see clearly enough that there is no
curve to the sea." And at the very same moment he was, without knowing it, following not a straight line but an arc of a
Great Circle. The man of common sense, before Galileo and
Kepler, believed that the heavens revolved around the Earth.
"You'd have to be mad," he would proclaim, "and ungodly too,
to think that the Earth, the center of creation, is nothing but a
fleck of mud revolving around the sun." And I, a man of common sense, am tempted to say today: "What folly, to believe
that the Universe is curved and circumscribed. This makes no
sense whatsoever." Which perhaps puts my reasoning on a level
with that of the Labrador duck.

At this point allow me a digression. This automatism of
thought also explains many political errors. Such and such a
statesman, although intelligent, when faced with certain problems will see no solution other than war because, in the past,
peoples always went to war when they found it impossible to
agree. Such and such a rebel, although intelligent, will see no
solution other than violent and armed revolution. Both are using
historical structures without realizing that the dimensions of the
phenomena and their nature have evolved. The very words they
use to think of public affairs have become inadequate. In the era
of radio and of television, democracy and news do not mean
the same things as they did in the days of Washington and
Jefferson. We are back to the thoughts of the Labrador duck.
The duck forgets that cement is not mud. The warmonger
forgets that nuclear warfare is not conventional warfare; the
revolutionary fails to realize that the state of the proletariat is

not what it used to be in Marx's time, and that today society can be transformed without bloody revolutions. Verbal illusions, those Bacon used to call *"idola fori,"* are among the most widespread.

Even science is not always successful in ridding itself of deeply implanted mental structures. The scientific genius is he who, all of a sudden, overthrows existing structures and introduces new ones. But, to achieve this, he has to overcome some of his own habits. Planck reluctantly put forward his quantum theory. Moreover the scientist who has made some extraordinary discovery, and has changed the science of his day, may become so obsessed with his own new findings that he will refuse to recognize those of his successors. His theory becomes, for him, an unbreakable habit, and even a point of honor.

An example of this: The biologist Metchnikoff, who gained fame for having demonstrated that the white cells of the blood, or phagocytes, swallow, absorb and destroy microbes, became so wedded to this theory that he erected it as a teleology; he persisted in seeing his phagocytes as the policemen of the body, entrusted by nature with the task of stopping the bacteria, those guilty invaders. When other, younger biologists proved that introducing antigens (animal or vegetable albumins, microbial toxins) into a living body produces antibodies which endow the organism with a certain degree of immunity before any action by the phagocytes, violent quarrels broke out between the partisans of the cellular theory of immunity and those of the humoral theory (action of the humors or body fluids). A renowned English physician, Wright, did his best to reconcile the two rival theories, stating that the antibodies modify the struc-

ture of the germs and facilitate their digestion by the phagocytes. From the Greek verb *opsonô* (I prepare food for),
Wright coined the name "opsonine" for the substance with
which the blood, having had the alarm signal, "would butter the
microbes for the phagocytes' meal." He conceived of measurable
opsonic indices which would allow the rational treatment of infectious diseases.

All this was pure illusion masquerading in the guise of scientific procedure. The opsonic indices had no practical value.
Wright, a man of integrity, finished by giving up this fallacious
theory in disgust, but for a long time he had been as attached to
it as Metchnikoff to his. We could cite many other cases of scientific obsessions, begetters of illusions. Until Pasteur appeared
spontaneous generation was a stubborn illusion. Freud and
Jung, along with the pure genius of their intuitions, let themselves be carried away, the former by his obsession with sexu-
ality, the latter by his, with archetypes.

In other words, a scientist is a man for all that. "The history
of the sciences," writes Louis de Broglie, "teaches us that the
mind of the scientist, like that of other men, is not devoid of a
certain measure of inertia. When a theory, that is to say a manner of foreseeing a category of phenomena, has proved successful, there is a tendency to stand by it and, considering it as
definitive, to refuse the effort of considering any others." It is
true that innovators almost always come up against strong resistance among our Labrador ducks. Fresnel, Maxwell, Einstein
were hard put to it to gain acceptance for the theories which
were to open broad new avenues to physics. I even got the impression that Louis de Broglie himself, in his most recent book,

puts up a certain degree of resistance to Heisenberg's relations of uncertainty. But in that case he has good reasons for exposing certain verbal illusions which lead to the adoption of excessive conclusions from accurate premises. We shall come back to this. In the meantime let us return to our central theme.

We have just been through the reservations which result in science being unable wholly to eliminate from among things, and to divest them of, the illusions due to man's weakness, to his inertia, to his traditional mental structures as well as to the conditions of experimentation. In the case of illusions proper, more stubborn than mere mistakes, even when man *knows,* even when the illusion has been explained to him, he continues to entertain it. The most outstanding philosopher cannot help seeing as crooked that straight stick, half in and half out of the water.

When a stone is thrown into a body of liquid the observer, if a layman, sees the resulting waves flowing along the surface, ever widening their circles. A better informed observer knows that the liquid particles move vertically, and that these displacements give the illusion of a circle in motion. He can calculate what happens at the meeting place of the waves, where the movements at times act in conjunction, at others cancel each other out and give an impression of immobility. He can explain how the waves are refracted by an obstacle. But however deep his science, if he just looks at the waves, he will see them flow. The difference is that if the scientist does remain subject to such illusions, he has broken down their mechanics. He knows that he cannot describe the world by making do with appearances only. Combining the crooked stick and the theory of refraction, he reaches a truer image. He does not suppress the illusion, but he does master it and integrate it. His method allows him to correct his impressions.

A hypothesis is never an illusion, even if later experiments prove that it was fallacious. It would be an illusion if the scientist were to persist in believing it true, despite evidence to the contrary; it is not an illusion if the researcher considers it a working hypothesis. "At the present stage of our knowledge," he says, "everything seems to confirm the truth of this hypothesis." But should some new experiment reveal tomorrow that the first hypothesis no longer explains the facts, we should immediately adopt the alternative. Newton's mechanics was an admirable working hypothesis and so remains at its own level, but the concept of the electromagnetic field eliminates one of its shortcomings, that of action from a distance. When Einstein showed that certain phenomena are intelligible only if the Newtonian theory is complemented by the two theories of relativity, and by the inclusion of the speed of light in equations leading to the determination of movement, he led one step further toward the elimination of the observer's illusions.

It would, however, be yet another illusion to believe that the theory of relativity is science's last word. Science will never issue any such last word. "We are relativists, of the quantic school, and to us Bohr's and Rutherford's fine mechanical structures seem almost like prehistoric gropings. Bohr's atom may still hold good for high school students; for us that era is already lost in the early dawn of discovery." * For the man of the year 2000 it is highly probable that the theories which satisfy us

* Leprince-Ringuet.

today will in turn have faded into the prehistoric ages. An illusion exists every time a researcher thinks he has found a definitive formula. As we have already observed, the history of science is a long series of mistakes and corrections. This is a subject neither for astonishment nor for regret. Hypotheses, although ever imperfect, are indispensable to research. "He who observes with no idea in mind, observes in vain." How can we conceive of, and elaborate, new experiments without a guide line? Our aim is to create new situations to confirm or to disprove the hypothesis.

There almost always comes a time when old hypotheses forgather with the moons of yesteryear. For close on to two hundred years combustion was explained by the presence within all bodies of a mysterious inflammable substance called phlogiston. Then Lavoisier showed that combustion was a chemical phenomenon, and phlogiston was relegated to the attic. For eighty years physicists believed in the existence of ether, an invisible, intangible element, the vehicle for light, for electricity and who knows what else. This idea was a useful one; then its usefulness disappeared. Was this an illusion? Yes, for all who believed in the real and absolute existence of ether; no, for those who considered ether as a temporarily convenient hypothesis.

Physics is in a state of constant change. At one time it defined light as the propagation of waves, which explained the phenomena of interference and diffusion. Further experiments revealed the existence of light corpuscles. These light quanta had to be included in the hypothesis, but without sacrificing the waves, which alone were compatible with the effects of interference. Louis de Broglie then imagined undulatory mechanics to bring together waves and corpuscles. The experimental method demands that the rich imagination of scientists should, upon occasion, give birth to such intuitions. When experiment contradicts a current theory another must needs be elaborated. Then this new theory, subject to the control of experimentation, will prevail until such time as still newer facts demand further revisions.

The gait of science is comparable to the gait of a parrot. Grasping the lowest rung of his cage with both feet, the bird reaches for an upper rung with his beak. When he has found it, he hangs on to it and then boldly lifts one foot to the level of his beak. When that position seems secure, he brings up the other foot and then repeats the exercise with his beak, and reaches upward to yet another rung. Science advances with the same circumspection as the parrot up his ladder, clinging to one hypothesis until it can safely grasp the next one.

The very matter of research changes. The conventional physicist used to raise no doubts with regard to the concrete nature of the real world. He either saw or touched what he was describing. The modern physicist studies particles which are in his view the elements of all reality, but are not directly observable. Yet he is sure of their existence, either because of their encounters with drops of water in Wilson's chamber, or because of the black or gray spot they produce on a photographic plate. When we see a long trail of white smoke in a cloudless sky, we say: "There's a jet plane passing overhead," although the plane itself is invisible. This might be an illusion. The white trail might be caused by some other phenomenon. At the present stage of our knowledge the presence of a plane remains the most probable hypothesis.

For long years physicists endeavored to imagine the atom by structuring it along the lines of other systems familiar to them, such as that of the planets around the sun. Electrons, forced to follow a definite orbit, revolved around a nucleus. If this nucleus was bombarded by particles something would break off from it. This led to the representation of the nucleus as an agglomeration of marbles held together by powerful forces. The bombardment released one marble. But the nucleus could just as well have been imagined as a drop of water. If you shake a large drop, it vibrates; add to the sum of energy by shaking it harder and the large drop will subdivide, and a smaller drop will become detached from it. Marbles and drops of water are but images; they help the human mind to understand. For our brain, formed by thousands of years of reaction to a visible world, needs such images. Illusions would step in if we were to assert that the atom *is* truly a planetary system, and the nucleus an agglomeration of marbles. "Images," said Henri Poincaré, "are but garments subject to all the vagaries of fashion." The true, the lasting theory is a system of relationships.

There are two ways of representing an object which neither our senses nor our instruments are capable of apprehending: by an image or by calculation. If we take the image for the event itself this, as we have said earlier, is an illusion. No image of the atom is satisfactory. The physics of the infinitely great and of the infinitely small discourage any attempt at concrete representation. The mind then seeks refuge in calculation. A particle is nothing more than the probable position of a field. But mathematics is only a tool. These convenient symbols cannot constitute reality itself. "I am deeply convinced," says Louis de Broglie, "of the existence of a physical reality exterior to ourselves, independent of our thought and of our imperfect means of seizing it." For years scientists considered this physical reality subject to laws. Then a later generation conceived the idea that these laws were statistical laws only, true on a macroscopic, inexistent on a microscopic, scale. This is where we find Heisenberg and his relationship of uncertainty. He states that at the level of microphysics, phenomena are undetermined. If so, a serious problem arises. Are we to conclude that, because the future position of a particle is unpredictable, scientific determinism was an illusion? Are we going to have to forgo this working hypothesis which yielded such prodigious results?

We may well wonder whether mathematical symbols, too, do not beget illusions. We place our confidence in this wonderful tool; these simplifications, these symmetrical formulae are a source of esthetic and intellectual pleasure. "But our attention is diverted from objects. . . . Just as a traveller emerging from a long tunnel suddenly discovers a new sky, a different countryside, so he who emerges from the mathematical underpass often finds himself face to face with astonishing conclusions which he cannot doubt but which he is not always able to explain by recourse to our usual concepts." Here we are back to an idea of Louis de Broglie's which I have already mentioned: that excessive conclusions may be drawn from accurate premises. It seems, for instance, excessive to use the indeterminate nature of particles as an argument in favor of human free will. I am not stating that free will is an erroneous concept; I say that the relationship between man's freedom and the indetermination of particles is not proven.

Another example: I am no great believer in the fantastic deductions that have been drawn from Einstein's theories. They raised wild hopes concerning Time, which all of a sudden was no longer relentless. People thought that it would be possible to slow down its passing flight, and to go backward into the past. You may remember the curious fable about relativity conceived by the French physicist Langevin: "This can supply any one of us willing to devote two years of his life to it, with the means of knowing what the Earth will be like two hundred years from now, of exploring the future of the Earth by means of a forward leap which will represent two centuries in the Earth's life, two years in his own. All that would be needed would be for our traveler to agree to being shut up in a missile to be projected from the earth at a speed reasonably close, though still inferior, to that of light, which is a physical possibility. The flight would be so organized that the missile would encounter a star at the end of one year of the traveler's life. This would project him back to the earth at the same speed. Back on earth again, older by two years, the traveler will emerge from his ark and find our globe older by two hundred years, provided that in the interval his speed had remained inferior by as little as one twenty-thousandth to that of light." And Langevin concluded boldly with the statement: "The most securely established facts of experimental physics allow us to assert that this is exactly what would take place."

This idea has supplied science-fiction writers with remarkable themes, but in spite of my respect for Langevin, his extrapolation does not appear to me to be justified. "Mathematical deductions, when applied to the order of realities, form a powerful instrument, but are subject to the general stipulation that the premises must be the results of observation, and the conclusions be checked against experiment." *

Einstein himself challenged the right of the mathematician to transpose certain surprising relationships into an image of the world. He refused to admit the surrender of determinism before probabilism. "God does not roll dice," he said. To this I can imagine others answering: "How right; God does not roll our human dice, for these have only six sides. But throughout an infinity of time He does roll *His own* dice which have an infinite number of sides." As a result of which less and less likely organizations come to light. The formation of the eye by means of the procedures of the selection and of the survival of the fittest seems inconceivable, because the probability of the fortuitous formation of so complex a system seems almost nil, but man does not extrapolate in the same way as nature does.

Sir James Jeans fancied an apologue to show that we are in danger of attributing to probability phenomena determined by causality pure and simple. In a two-dimensional universe live absolutely flat larvae. From time to time showers fall onto the plane which constitutes their universe. Our flat larvae which, lacking a third dimension, cannot conceive of rain, see parts of their world become moist, then dry again, and do not understand the nature of these wet patches. A mathematically inclined larva then proves that it is impossible to foresee when a patch will disappear, or when it will reappear at some unpredictable spot. But it applies to this phenomenon the rule of probabilities, obtains creditable results and is awarded the larvae's Nobel Prize. Yet the phenomenon *rain,* which alone could afford an

* Berthelot. Letter to Renan.

accurate explanation, escapes the larva's understanding. Does it not seem possible, and even probable, that essential elements of our own universe escape our knowledge? For thousands of years men thought of the world as a privileged location, created by a specific decree of Providence. For thousands of years men knew nothing of electricity, of hertzian waves, of radiation; they existed none the less. For thousands of years they enjoyed the heat of the sun unaware of radioactivity, and without seeking a rational explanation for that heat. There seems little reason to doubt that we live among prodigious sources of energy of whose very existence we have no inkling. The notion of a universal science was an illusion of the seventeenth, eighteenth and nineteenth centuries.

We have given up their image of the Universe (as Laplace conceived it) as a giant machine so well ordered that, knowing the position of all its parts at instant t, we should be able to predict their position at instant t', just as it is possible in a planetarium to relocate the stars in their precise position the night that Christ was born. On the other hand we continue to believe that within a self-contained system, and on a certain scale, the physicist is indeed able to predict what will come to pass. Failing which there would be no engineers, no science, no industry. But we recognize with Heisenberg that there is a realm of determinism and one of indeterminism. We recognize that, at this stage of our knowledge, we are unable to predict the fate of one individual particle, and still less, when life is involved, the fate of one cell; or if society is involved, the fate of one human being; or in the realm of history, the future of nations.

Indeed, a trait common to all living beings is that they are unpredictable. An amoeba moves, but we are incapable of describing its movements in advance. As to man we cannot reduce him to a mere machine. Cybernetics reproduces almost all of man's mechanical actions, can contrive an artificial hand or heart, can even produce an artificial mathematician or pilot. In its mechanical world it reproduces the selection of the fittest. The automobile replaces the horse because the automobile is the better adapted. The Automobile Show is very like a phase of the struggle for life. Third generation computers eliminate the primitive models. Only the very best survive. But cybernetics cannot endow its robots with consciousness. It is able to manufacture a life-guard robot capable of saving a drowning swimmer. It could even endow its machine with a device that will respond to the drowning man's shout for help, and follow the direction of these sounds. It is quite incapable of inspiring the robot with the will to save the swimmer, to endow it with pity and brotherly love. Properly speaking, human dimensions have notably shrunk. Machines have gained ground. It is none the less true that there remains an area which cannot be explained. We have every right to believe that this zone too will, sooner or later, be mastered. We have no right to assert it.

Computers are stupid. They can carry out only the simplest mathematical operations; but they do so at such speed that they resolve problems much faster than the human brain. Our brain can store up far more information than the machine but is less skilful at sorting, recalling and using it. The brain is the better by reason of its amazingly minute dimensions, but it is probable that computers too will be reduced to minute size. It is also probable, and I would venture to say certain, that computers will reproduce, and that one computer will design the blueprint of a more highly perfected model. Quite certainly a computer learns by its own mistakes and is able to point out and to correct man's errors. Is it capable of autonomous thought, that is to say, of possessing consciousness? I do not think so, but then who can tell? The computer is a sociologist, a psychologist. Can it become a metaphysician? Some time ago I dreamt up the following story:

A scholar believes that he has discovered the unique formula which will provide the key to the universe. Lengthy mathematical operations must still be carried out. The scholar feeds the questions to a computer. While the machine is hard at work, the scholar dies. The machine goes on, churning out a thousand operations per second, producing miles of paper covered with figures which no one is left to interpret. All the disciples are there, voiceless, disconsolate; they believe that the solution is almost within their reach, that the key to the universe is about to be revealed, but that they will be unable to grasp it. Then, suddenly, the machine comes to a halt; then it prints these three letters: G. O. D. Please do not be alarmed. This is pure fiction. But I have the feeling that Einstein would have enjoyed it.

Just as soon as living beings and, *a fortiori,* men are involved, the importance of interpretation, and hence of illusions, increases. The computer is of great value to the sciences of life for the mechanical or statistical aspects of research concerning them. However Doctor Dubois, delivering a Pegram Lecture in this hall, told you that life differs in many ways from what we know of the inanimate world. For instance in the case of an inert system entropy is constantly on the increase, whereas living orga-

nisms, starting off with inanimate components, maintain an order which vanishes the moment life ceases. As for the mind,
whatever its nature, we face the fact that to this day no one has
succeeded in totally reducing it to physico-chemical phenomena.
The belief that this is possible is an illusion dear to more than a
few; it is not a scientific truth.

Let us consider medicine for instance. For a long time it par-
took more of magic than of science. Many an intelligent man,
and indeed many physicians, used to consider its prescriptions
and its diagnostics as illusions. "Give nature a little leeway," said
Montaigne; "she knows her business better than we." As late as
the nineteenth century, Magendie, an eminent physiologist,
placed little reliance on therapeutics. He used to say to his in-
terns: "It is easy to see that you have never tried not to intervene
at all," and to those who would suggest a treatment: "If you feel
like it, why not? Go ahead." In the early years of our own century skeptics, influenced by their shattered enthusiasms, asserted
that medicine was a matter of fashion. Colloidal metals had
been used for the treatment of infections. Influenza had been
cured with silver and tuberculosis with tin. Illusions these! Who
even remembers them? Once out of fashion the medication
would no longer cure. And wouldn't there be a strange romance
to write under the title *Decline and Fall of Cholesterol?*

This climate of skepticism and of illusions has completely
changed. Vaccines and serums, sulfonamides and antibiotics,
transfusions and grafts, how could we lack faith in the presence
of all these miracles? The practitioner of our day has at his
disposal a formidable arsenal of arms against disease of which
his forerunners had no inkling. Chemistry, electronics, radi-

ology, isotopes, biology lead him into what was before virgin territory. But have these triumphant achievements dispelled all the causes of illusion? Have they changed medicine into an exact science? It appears to me that medical activity in our day is drawing closer to scientific activity, without however wholly merging with it. The physician makes generous use of the data supplied by science. But there remain broad divergences between him and the chemist or the biologist.

First and foremost the scientific researcher wants to be sure of the truth of his hypotheses. He seeks to eliminate all subjective factors. He will repeat his experiments a hundred times over to avoid any chance of error; he will go on until he has conceived and put into practice the crucial experiment that will dispel every last doubt. While the physician cannot afford to wait. "The purpose of medicine is action, not perfection." The danger of a mistaken diagnosis is great; far greater is the danger of letting the patient die for lack of treatment. In the absence of any characteristic syndrome it is the physician's duty to trust his intuition and take bold action. Best of them all is he who at one and the same time calls upon his science, his experience and his knowledge of men. Charity is not an essential virtue for the physicist or the chemist; it is indispensable for the physician and for the surgeon alike.

We can imagine a diagnostic machine to which a laboratory would supply on punch cards all the data concerning a patient's condition. Actually such machines exist today; they are useful because they absorb and sort, within seconds, more factors than the human brain can master. If the symptoms are precise enough the machine will, thanks to its prodigious memory, recall some very rare disease which the practitioner would not have thought of. But in a complex case will it come to as sure a conclusion as the great clinician? How could we admit this? The machine is unable to establish a hierarchy among symptoms. For that matter not all data are measurable or transmittable. If the physician fails to take the imponderables into account, he runs the risk of losing his soul—and his patient.

Statistics, to be sure, allow an accurate forecast of what will happen to a large group of patients; they help to measure the degree of risk and thereby to make a decision in theory. But statistics do not permit any forecast with respect to the evolution of an individual case, and "of what avail is it to the doomed individual that some other shall go on living in his place in order to bring statistical tables back to their norms?" The physician is one specific patient's doctor. If the patient trusts him the doctor becomes a living remedy whose very presence is salutary, "a remedy among the ingredients of which we find an alkaloid called love or charity." * An illusion? Perhaps, but a beneficent illusion. Upon the arrival of his doctor the patient calms down and soon the thermometer "like one of the three Fatal Sisters, overcome by a more powerful god, brings its silver spindle to a halt." The mind has cured the body. Well aware of the unity of the human person, the complete physician extends his treatment to despair, to illusions and to the organic ills they beget.

What is important for our subject is that, reaching the science of man, we are entering an area where interpretation plays at the very least as important a part as research, and this once more opens the door to illusions.

* Chauchard.

Let us consider another of the sciences of man. Economics too is still in that borderland which divides magic and science; it has had its triumphs, it may offer some degree of certainty, but it remains a very gallery of illusions. Karl Marx wrote: "In the realm of political economy, free scientific research encounters not only the same foe as in other branches. The specific nature of the matter with which it deals allies against it the most violent, the most tawdry, the most malevolent passions which stir the human breast, that is to say the furies of personal interests. Thus the Anglican Church will forgive attacks against thirty-eight of its thirty-nine Articles of Faith rather than one attack against the thirty-ninth part of its revenues."

Here indeed, far more so than in physics, passions and interests come into play. If you prove to a liberal economist that the slump in securities in the stock market is such that the shares are quoted far below the value of realizable assets, he will answer: "That is an accident; the laws of the market will restore a proper balance." And then this balance is not restored within the time foreseen. Why? Because in a great many minds there was a breakdown in the mechanics of confidence. Confidence is not a measurable phenomenon. It is difficult to revive, the causes of its decrease varying from one individual to the next. Political passions come into play. "If geometry were as bound up with our interests as economics, geometrical truth would be the subject of virulent controversy."

For over a thousand years any loan bearing interest was considered in Europe as a sin. The theory of usury claimed that interest was a theft, since money is incapable of reproducing. As a concept that was completely absurd. If money is used in a

commercial enterprise, if it is invested in the purchase of a
machine, it produces goods which, without it, would not have
been created. Money represents objects which the investor goes
without in order to permit the production of other objects. But
for centuries this disastrous and stubborn illusion established
banking as a monopoly in the hands of those who did not share
it and forced the Italian bankers to dissimulate the nature of
their loans under transparent fictions.

Marx entertained the illusion of having discovered a major
cause of injustice when he exposed the confiscation by the
management of the surplus value produced by the workman,
over and above the wages of his work. To recognize such increase in value as an illusion all we need do is to consider two
firms, each of them employing equally skilled workers of the
same trade. One of these firms will be in the black, the other in
the red. Why? Because the first is well, the other badly, man-
aged. So what is the source of the surplus value? It springs from
the intelligence or the hard work of the managers. Injustice may
exist; it often does, but its cause is different. Yet the idea of surplus value remains an article of faith. Certain facets of economics are scientific; others are still theological. Marxism, for
some people, is an intelligent report on the England of 1840; for
others it is a religion.

For years and years economics was burdened with a Keynes-
ian illusion: the belief that the volume of currency in circulation
could be arbitrarily controlled. This illusion led to the acceptance of unbalanced budgets, to inflation and to depressions. It
held a strong attraction for governments, since it relieved them
of the need for prudence.

In politics as in economics men have blind spots within their fields of vision. They fail to see what they do not want to see. This is a negative illusion. In 1936 it was obvious to any rational human being that if France and England allowed Hitler to re-establish the military occupation of the Rhineland, war would swiftly follow. But the two governments clung to their illusions. They refused to see.

At times, when their political passions are involved, scientists themselves completely forget their scientific methods. During the war I heard a great physicist assert "facts" which, to my certain knowledge, were not true (that the French fleet had been turned over to the Germans, when it had, on the contrary, scuttled its own vessels). These were "facts" for which he could not possibly have had any evidence, but they came to the support of his political prejudices. A stubborn scientist, Lysenko, out of pure passion, was responsible for long delays in the progress of biology in the Soviet Union.

If minds well versed in critical and precise patterns of thought can so give rein to their illusions, what can be expected from humanity in the mass? An almost total incapacity for discerning between truth and error. At a time when we entertain hopes that the scientific mind will help men to agree on objective data, ignorance and superstition are stronger than ever. Astrologers, fortune tellers, crystal ball gazers continue to flourish. Quantities of apparently normal men and women check their horoscopes daily, buy lottery tickets, gamble and bet week after week, although the law of probabilities proves that sooner or later they are sure to lose, automatically, what with house rake-offs and state taxes. Apart from certain privileged groups, experimental scientific patterns of thought have not even begun to permeate general behavior.

Some say: "It's a bit science's fault. Science will calculate most precisely the microscopic course of a meson during its brief existence, but ignores the need for a general agreement on the conditions required for a healthy currency." Yes, but the meson does not run counter to man's secret desires, while the currency affects his daily life. All the more reason for applying scientific thought to the problem, but experiments in economic matters are not easily carried out. Such phenomena go well beyond the spread of a human lifetime. One generation's setbacks are forgotten by the next. So statistics are brought in. All well and good, but when statistical data imply an influence on politics, illusions once more rear their heads. A physicist will, without prejudice, measure the mass of a particle; a biologist will, with a relatively free mind, observe the data for the microbial population of a culture broth; but a pair of politicians will bombard each other with contradictory statistics. I myself have heard, on French television, a cabinet minister and a member of the opposition discussing the number of homes built during the preceding year. The member of the opposition claimed that this figure had notably decreased; the minister proved, with a wealth of statistics, that it had just as notably increased. The key to all this: one was talking in terms of percentages; the other in absolute terms and, in the final analysis, each of the two men was speaking about himself and about his election. If observation can modify phenomena, it can in far greater measure modify statistics, often in perfectly good faith. The way a question is put elicits the answer. Approaching the man in the street, I once personally rechecked a poll which, we were told, had revealed that 19 per cent of the French population were favorable to a certain measure; rewording the question, I found 2 per cent.

Politics is still far removed from scientific methods. A French professor, Monsieur Fourastié, claims all too accurately that the average man understands less and less about the nature of science. "The weakness of his scientific understanding and the misconception of scientific techniques are such that, however deeply he may deplore it, the average man can conceive only of force to resolve political conflicts. 'No progress without struggle' remains a tenet adopted by right wing and left wing alike, and by that they mean physical strife, not intellectual effort, not scientific enquiry into the optimum conditions for the nation. The consequences of this lack of faith in scientific methods govern the entire social and political climate of this age." The average man still adheres to the traditional methods of contention.

It is a dangerous illusion to believe that historical analogies can serve to forecast the future. Analogy is not the same as identity. Circumstances are never exactly the same. For years politicians were obsessed by memories of Munich and Yalta. The conclusion was that the slightest attempt at appeasement or conciliation was a mistake. The expression "Another Munich" would damn any negotiation. But it is often wise to negotiate. Hitler's blind folly is not a permanent historical factor. Should a country, just because of Munich, go to war every time it finds itself in conflict with a foreign power? Or should it seek a compromise? The projection of past memories onto future events cannot supply the answer. Everything depends upon an objective appraisal of the present factors of the problem.

The historian is not, like the physicist, a scientist, the dis-
coverer of immutable laws; he is more akin to the doctor, whose
diagnosis is accurate because his long experience has endowed
him with a kind of flair. In history we find recurring structures.
In their early days revolutions are often ruthless and fanatical.
They commit excesses which shock the majority of the citizens.
There comes a time when either the violent elements must be
curbed or a counter-revolution be undergone. The historian
recognizes these symptoms. Still he must take into account the
nature of the patient. Mao Tse-tung is neither Stalin nor Robespierre. There is no such thing as the science of history. "We advance toward the future with backward tread," said Paul Va-
léry. We advance toward the future with our faces turned to
the past. But the statesman must have a care not to project his
historical passions upon an unforeseeable future.

Would it be possible, for that matter, even if men were sin-
cerely willing, to reach solutions acceptable to all concerned? Is
there not the illusion of the Fellow-man, which leads us to
imagine this other as similar to ourselves? But he is *not* similar
to us. Just because *we* see a multi-colored world we believe that
all creatures see these colors. Not at all. Birds and insects do distinguish between different colors, but mammals, man excepted,
see objects as black or white, and this includes the bull. He
charges the matador's cape not because it is red, but because it
moves. When we talk with a color-blind person, he does not
complain about his infirmity. He uses the terms "red" and
"green." We have no idea of what he means by these words.
Just as color does not exist for certain beings, so morality or at
any rate our morality does not exist for certain types. In a recent

article Lord Eccles said that for a major part of British youth, Christian morality is no longer an accepted value. What could we propose as the basis for a common policy?

In the eighteenth century philosphers thought and taught that politics and economics would soon be governed by Newton's methods. Rational politics could not fail to take sway. Rousseau, Montesquieu, Condorcet, Locke and Jefferson were convinced of this. The generation of 1780 hoped that they had so thoroughly destroyed despotism that never again would freedom and justice be imperiled. This was a wave of pride and faith which seemed natural after certain recent triumphs of reason. But men remained men, and their passions were to reopen the whole question.

Today we have less confidence in the future than the man of a hundred years ago. Renan, in 1863, wrote to Berthelot: "Who knows but that man may succeed in learning the last word about matter, the laws of life, the laws of the atom? Who can tell whether, having mastered the secrets of matter, a predestined chemist may not transform all things? Who can tell whether, having mastered the secrets of life, an omniscient biologist may not modify its conditions, whether some day all natural species will not appear to us as the relics of a clumsy, out of date world, the remains to be kept, for curiosity's sake, in our museums? Who knows, in short, whether infinite science will not bring with it infinite power? . . . He who shall possess such science will verily be the master of the universe. Since for him space will no longer exist, he will transcend the boundaries of his own planet. One single power will truly govern the world and that will be science, that will be the mind."

We must admire Renan's prescience, for the laws of the atom, transmutation, the modification of genes, man's great leap into space—all these, in 1863, were in the far distant future but already present to his mind. However better informed than he and more powerful, we are infinitely more modest. We no longer believe that infinite knowledge will make us masters of the Universe. We do not believe that the world will be governed by our science. We do not believe that we shall ever discover nature's last secret. We believe that any such last secret is the supreme illusion. Our brain is equipped not for any such enterprise as this but rather for supplying us with an image of the world useful to the individual within the limited scope of his *Lebensraum*. We occupy within this Universe a space so minute that it would be foolhardy to speak of a totality of which we cannot even conceive. Traveling to the Moon will be an astounding feat, but how does that compare to the distances between us and the outer galaxies? Even were we to learn that our Universe is finite, may there not be at inconceivable distances other universes so far away that our instruments do not react to them? And if we turn to the opposite infinity, that of particles, no sooner do we explore this Universe than we destroy it. We are, it has been said, like a blind man trying to grasp snowflakes, whose presence was revealed to him by some mysterious intuition. As soon as he draws near, the heat of his breath makes them melt. Far from understanding more and more, he understands less and less. "We know," said Oppenheimer, "that we are, and that we shall remain ignorant."

Although science has made incredible progress, although man is able, from thousands of miles away, to exert influence on a tiny device moving in infinite space, although he has begun to conceive of the mechanics of life and may hope that some day his action upon the genes will allow him to modify his own being, although he has increased the average life span from twenty-five to seventy-five years, we know that we know nothing. The layman entertains the illusion that science has an answer to all questions. The scientist does not share this illusion.

Our layman is particularly partial to another general illusion: that science can bring happiness to all men. Science does indeed make available to us superabundant energy, means of production and machines that may improve the human estate. Indeed, even if our science is still imperfect, it is, at our level, extremely powerful and satisfies many of our needs. Indeed science frees man from heavy labor and irksome tasks. Indeed in countries such as ours hunger, cold and darkness have been overcome—or almost. Indeed less work produces greater comfort. But this is not true for a vast area of our planet, where the increase in population outstrips the increase in food supplies.

Furthermore, the vast forces of science are not often applied to the most urgent needs. A great physician once told me: "I used to think that if I could establish contact with the top decision-making echelons, I should be able to ensure better use of the forces of science. So I told the high civil servants responsible for the French Economic Plan that cancer could be eradicated if sufficient funds were allocated to cancer research. I was given two billion francs, while space research got seventy. I then asked myself two questions, and supplied my own answers: Out of fifty million Frenchmen, how many will die of cancer? At least ten million. How many will go to the moon? Perhaps none;

perhaps ten. Well? The retort was: 'Yes, but by virtue of the principle of reversibility, efforts to reach the moon will result in the means of curing cancer.' I said, in turn: 'Perhaps; but by virtue of the same principle, the study of cancer may teach us how man may live on the moon.'"

It is quite true that in many directions scientists could cure men of illusions as dangerous as they are ancient. One example: Since the beginning of time women have had the illusion that they must bring forth in pain and suffering. Then the physicians told them: "No! Put your brains to better use; master your reflexes and you will give birth without pain." And it turned out to be true. Our brain is an admirable machine, put to very poor use. There should be a world board of scientists to meet from time to time and examine the long and the short term consequences of inventions. I believe that this is already being done. But this board has no power to ban the use of harmful discoveries. The decision is in the hands of small groups, that is, governments, and the governments, in turn, are subject to public opinion.

But this opinion, the product of average human beings, is unable to understand that the scientific approach, a prodigiously efficient merger of intuition and experience, would be capable of organizing both politics and economics infinitely superior to those practiced by the countries of the world. The voter, the citizen lets himself be swayed by anger or by enthusiasm. How can we advise a politician, whose only ambition is to win or to keep his seat, to exert the prudence, the good faith, the patience demanded by experimental methods? He would laugh at any such egghead. For him politics is an adventure. His are the methods of publicity, not of science.

Apart from a few, very rare, wise men, swept up onto the shores of history by some great tidal wave, most of the great leaders of men were players, acting out their own parts. Napoleon, a man of genius, well able to understand the scientific mind, surrounded by scholars of his own choice, strutted the stage when he met with the Emperor of Russia, and when he gave himself up to the English. If such are the frailties of a great man, can we be surprised when the average man, with dramatic gestures and fine words, plunges into the stormy waters instead of steering a scientific course? "War is the last word of passion," said Alain. "One and all were just waiting for such an opportunity. There is no real peace when the lover dreams only of punishing his faithless lover, the rich man of punishing the poor, and the poor man the rich. . . . Who can fail to realize the power of this collective passion, when all the rage fostered by ambition, by disease, by old age, finds such satisfactory expression, to the tune of general approval and accompanied by glory? Who can fail to see how imitation of others and self-respect plunge the best of our youth into the vortex, while precocious passions even more readily plunge the worst?"

How indeed, after such delirium, can we counsel scrupulous experiments and integrity of mind? The man of violence laughs at facts. "It is far easier to die for a cause than to appraise its righteousness through observation and experiment." That is why we are nowhere near achieving experimental politics. On the field of battle men follow in Illusion's footsteps, their courage as unconscious as it is heroic, and march off to their death or future misery with a song on their lips.

Let us suppose that more and more highly perfected computers should be able to predict, unerringly, the effects of a nuclear war. Let us suppose that Mao Tse-tung should be scientifically certain that such a war would spell the end of his country and of the human race. Let us suppose that every Chinese, every Russian, every American should share this scientific certainty. Do you believe that this would be a guaranty against the folly of mankind? I do not believe it. It was both certain and obvious that the war of 1939 would spell the ruin of Europe. It was both certain and obvious that it would result in immense and pointless calamities. And yet the war took place. It was both certain and obvious that the Maginot Line could be outflanked. And yet that Line inspired confidence. Everything is yet to be done before mankind can be invested with even the rudiments of the scientific mind. Everything is yet to be done "to create a new human being, one who does not love war, who feels no inexorable urge to hate foreigners, to torture the weak, to make the innocent pay." Everything is yet to be done. And yet we must try. For there would lie our salvation.

When, in his presence, his sons indulged in arguments as fiery as they were futile over political and economic questions, the great British statesman Lord Salisbury would say to them: "You must think of this chemically." He was right. If men, or at least the best among them, would learn to consent to scientific discipline, to submit their decisions to the test of experiment and to accept nature's answers, politics and economics would follow a less perilous path. To be sure experiment would, in many cases, still prove impossible. In such an event the political genius would have to rely on intuitive decisions, but even for the genius the very fact of being trained in the rigor, the circumspection and the integrity of scientific methods would be an invaluable safeguard against dangerous illusions. By purging perceptions of their individual factors science makes the human mind, in every branch of its action, a more precise and a more efficient tool.

Now let us return to the questions we put at the beginning of this address. *Does science free man from his illusions?* Yes; in its own domain objective observation corrects the errors of our senses, experiments confirm or invalidate our hypotheses, illusions are overcome, the gods have been driven from the rivers and the woods, the stars and the mountain tops. But just as soon as experiment becomes impossible, either because the phenomena are too complex, or because it would demand a period of time stretching beyond the limits of one seeker's life, just so soon does illusion find its way back into the mental process.

Is science itself without illusions? We have seen that the scientist, being a man, is not wholly impervious to illusions. He does, upon occasion, accept as a truth that which satisfies his mind. But it is by no means sure that the world obeys the same laws of esthetics or symmetry as the human mind. The greatest scientist knows but one tree of a mighty forest; he entertains an illusion when he thinks he can speak of the forest. Lastly there are cases when the scientist, unconsciously, goes from hypothesis to flat statement. His pride then establishes a permanent link between his own personality and temporary solutions. However the great man of science, he who is imbued with the truly scientific spirit, voids the world of all that is personal to himself and achieves impartiality toward his own theories.

Can illusions survive in an age of science and technology?

The proof of their survival is, as we have said, that soothsayers and astrologers make a handsome living, that politics remains a web of illusions and that the novel keeps its readers. That is easy to understand. Certain events can, thanks to science, be foretold, but the future, as a whole, remains unpredictable. And what man would most wish to foretell is precisely what eludes experiment: love, happiness, death, genius. It is natural, science supplying no answers to these questions, that man should turn to magic, to daydreams and to hope; it is natural that, in place of science, faith in art should step in. Technical progress cannot, by itself, determine moral changes. "Things are not so simple, and the structure of human societies is also dependent upon feelings and thoughts and indeed upon poetry which awaits but some degree of leisure to dream and to sing its songs upon our thresholds."

We shall see, in the last lecture, what the fine arts can offer to man.

Wilful Illusions or the Fine Arts

HERE WE enter a universe entirely different from that of science. The scientist strives to dispel illusions; he reduces them to an ever narrower margin of error; he seeks to reach an objective reality, which may be grasped through the medium of phenomena and is measurable. The artist, on the contrary, strives to create illusions. That is his trade. "I call a creator," says Schiller, "the man who can so project his state of sensitivity upon an object that this object, in turn, constrains us, the spectators, to partake of that same state of sensitivity." In other words the artist must be as subjective as the scientist is objective, while giving us the illusion that his subjectivity and ours are one and the same.

For instance, if the artist is a novelist, he builds an imaginary world of his own (the worlds of Flaubert, Proust, Hemingway, Faulkner) which he strives to make us share. The astonishing thing about this operation is that the artist knows that this world is illusory, since it is his creation, and that we, readers or spectators, know it too. No one, unless he be a primitive or a child, believes that the drama acted out on a stage is real; no one, when reading a novel, is unaware of its being the novelist's creation. Indeed, neither the canvas nor the novel copy life. Art demands great sacrifices. The painter sacrifices the third dimension, the novelist the stretch of time. The illusion is wilful. Why then do author, reader, spectator take such lively pleasure in deceiving themselves? We shall endeavor first to expound the point of view of the audience, then that of the artist, after which we shall seek to determine whether the artist can survive in the technological and industrial society of our day.

First, it is a fact that the illusions of art have always played and still play a preponderant part in the lives of human societies. Remember how deeply affected all peoples were when the artistic treasures of Florence, or Venice, were threatened. A great work of art is part of a universal heritage. The Mona Lisa is invited to Washington on an official visit, the Venus of Milo to Tokyo. As far back as we may reach into the past, men have always been painters, sculptors, poets. They have always invented legends and myths. The cave dwellers used to draw animals on their walls. In the South Seas the most savage islanders sang, danced and painted their totem poles with the purest pigments. In ancient Egypt tombs, upon which no human eye was supposed to fall, were adorned with splendid bas-reliefs and paintings. Homer's epics expressed the cultural unity of ancient Greece, the Gothic cathedrals the unity of medieval Europe. As to our modern world, men buy paperback editions of novels by the million, visit museums in serried ranks and, at the movies or on television, watch dramas that they know are works of fiction. Why? Why do states and cities take it upon themselves to provide, in museums and libraries, impressive homes for artificially created worlds? Why is artistic illusion just as respected as scientific truth?

If we give it some thought, nothing could be stranger. In life we are surrounded by houses, trees, fruit, human bodies, and yet we join the crush at the doors of an exhibition to gaze upon distorted reproductions of these very objects or beings. We are, daily, tormented or elated by desire, jealousy, ambition and, instead of forgetting human suffering in our leisure hours, we go to watch, on stage or screen, dramas similar to our own. Again, why? Is real life not rich enough, good enough or evil enough to satisfy us or to dishearten us?

Several answers come to mind. The first is that we demand of art what life cannot give us. When we violently desire something, there are two ways of soothing our emotion. One is to acquire or to master what we desire; this is action. A savage is hungry; he goes fishing or hunting. A young man wants a woman; he woos her or takes her by force. But action may be impossible. Some men are too weak to pursue game or women. Others are starving in a region where no game passes, or are hot with desire in a fortress where no woman ever sets foot. In such cases what is the reaction of human beings?

They pass from action to representation, from reality to illusion. What does the primitive hunter do when he cannot find the bison or the reindeer he is all for killing and eating? He draws the animal on the stony walls of his cave and obscurely hopes that the image will conjure up the game. Worried about his crops, impatiently waiting for spring, what does the primitive plowman do? He dances the dance of spring; he leaps into the air to encourage the cornstalks to leap out of the ground. In all agricultural civilizations we find spring festivals and sun myths in which the resurrection of the god, after a long winter, becomes the symbol of resurgent verdure.

Unconsciously every one of us practices these imitative magic rites. In the front seat of a car, next to a reckless driver, our muscles contract and at every dangerous curve we slam on an imaginary foot brake. This is a futile, inoperative act, but it relieves our nervous tension. We are dancing the dance of the chauffeur, like the savage dancing the dance of spring. When you watch a tennis match or a football game, if your team fails to execute the moves which would spell victory, your excitement becomes so great that you get up from your seat and act them out yourself. You are dancing the football player's dance. Art, for the cave painter, was a substitute for activity; it still is for many readers of novels and motion picture fans. Erotic films are the preferred fare of those who have no erotic life. Science fiction comforts those who expect from science miracles that science is not yet able to produce. Illusion is the complement of reality.

This first explanation of art embraces part of the truth; it obviously remains quite inadequate. It is not because we feel a frustrated desire for three apples and a rickety table that we admire one of Cézanne's still lifes. Men and women who are by no means frustrated, whose love life seems admirably full, happy and adjusted none the less enjoy a beautiful love story. Napoleon took pleasure in rereading the tragedies of Corneille. This was certainly not for any lack of tragic circumstances in his own life. Why then do we seek refuge in wilful illusions when the real world affords us so many and such intense emotions? Why are those who see in art nothing more than the means of creating touching incidents actually second-rate artists? We must approach the problem from a different angle.

Imagine the streets of a town teaming with a huge and leaderless crowd. This happens in panics and riots. The mass swirls and surges about. Women faint; children scream. It is a chaotic and terrifying sight. Why? Because they all feel the presence of a colossal force upon which no order is exerted, because the movements of the crowd are unpredictable, because the mass itself does not know what it will do next. Every one of its members has an impression of anxiety and of terror.

On the other hand imagine the same number of human beings on the Champs-Elysées or on Fifth Avenue the day of a victory parade or of a hero's funeral. No anxiety, no terror. Why? Because this crowd is orderly. Lined up along the sidewalks the bystanders themselves define the route of the procession. Its own existence provides the crowd with the prologue to the show. A ceremony, its movements planned and prepared, changes the crowd into a work of art. The soldier on parade enjoys a feeling of fulfilment. He is part of an intelligible order. Ceremonies are one of the earliest art forms. The drama was first a religious ritual. What are Shakespeare's heralds and trumpets, his kings followed by their courts, the two scenes of the Holy Grail in Parsifal, if not ceremonies?

And what are the first movements of architecture if not ceremonies expressed in stone? The triumphal arch towers above and frames the triumphal march. Before ever one was built by an architect, the lines of the stadium were drawn by the crowds sitting on the slopes of the hillside. We are impressed by the simple beauty of these monuments, the symbols of accepted order. In our terrifying universe (for so it remains, in spite of, sometimes because of, science) order brings with it the possibility of understanding a more humane world. "Beauty," says Kant, "is what may be understood without concept." A seemingly obscure sentence, but one which arch, stadium and cathedral illuminate. The concepts of theology are arduous and abstract, but the spires of Chartres or the towers of Notre Dame raise heavenwards the thoughts of the simplest and even of the most doubting souls.

Let us take another example. A man dies suddenly, at home. He is on the floor where he fell, his limbs are limp and in disarray, his mouth is twisted, his lips are bloodied. The family is in tears. What have human societies invented to relieve such painful tensions? They lay the dead man on his bed; they fold his hands upon his breast. What is the meaning of all this if not that they are already carving a sculpture, the recumbent figure for the tomb, and changing the deceased into a work of art? Then they go to their church, their chapel or their temple. There they chant prayers, in which the orderliness of music provides a setting for their sighs and their sobs. A procession forms and sets out toward the grave. All funeral marches are slow, with a strong beat, to help bring the passions under control. Thanks to this illusory world, to the music and to the ceremony, grief little by little finds its place within the social order and takes on a strange, sad beauty.

A raging crowd, a tragic death, these are extreme cases, but we know that in his daily life man is ever, to a greater or a lesser degree, hagridden. Even when all goes well, all does not go perfectly well. Life remains, on the face of it, absurd. What is the meaning of this strange carnival? Why are we here on this fleck of mud, revolving in darkness? Why do our acts carry in their wake unexpected results? We want peace, concord and the affection of other peoples, and lo and behold here we are at war, massacring and being massacred. Or again we are in love with a woman who at times seems to love us in return and, at others, for no reason known to us, grows cold and distant. We do not understand the universe; we do not understand those who hate us; we do not understand those who love us; often we do not even understand our own parents, our children. We do not understand ourselves. Why did we take this or that deplorable decision? Why can we not find, at least within ourselves, that unity which we fail to find outside us? At times we feel so exhausted by the struggle that we dream of an intelligible universe, of a world in which men and women, things and symbols would no longer be unanswerable enigmas. But does such a world exist?

It does exist. It is the world of art. In this imaginary world there are conflicts just as in the real world, but these conflicts are not painful, nor are they without cure. Consider great music for instance. In its indirect and mysterious way it expresses our own emotions. It carries within it grief, laments and joy. In the first movement of Beethoven's Fifth Symphony two themes are opposed: a solemn warning of Fate, those four far-famed strokes of doom, and a lighter, more worldly theme. The entire movement is a conflict between these two themes; it ends with their reconciliation. The prelude to Tannhäuser is a conflict between the sacred theme of the Pilgrims and the profane theme of the Venusberg; at the end of the prelude the two themes converge and merge. The conflict is resolved. In music there are storms, tempests of sounds and emotions which at times overwhelm the audience; but the music, in its order, brings storm and tempest under control, and this gives us the illusion of a victory over the disorder of the world.

What is the secret of the order in music? It is first the alternation and the recurrence of strong and weak tempi. Rhythm is always reassuring to the human mind because it makes anticipation possible. The infant stops crying when its mother dances it up and down, rocks it or fondles it. Musical rhythm brings us the same reassurance as the rocking of its cradle brings to the infant. All music, from the most primitive to the most sophisticated, from songs to symphony, exists only through combinations of rhythm and the recurrence of themes which give the listener the joy of recognition and allow him, to a certain extent, to anticipate. But "to a certain extent" only. The theme recurs modulated, transposed, different. It is a pleasure for the intellect, when we listen to a quartet, to follow a theme as it goes from cello to violin; to hear the musicians pass it along, from one to the other, ingeniously varying it on its way, only to meet in the finale, all four repeating the theme in unison and with superb mastery. Another more secret order derives from the mathematical relationships between the notes, the chords and the harmonics. And this well-ordered world, although rich in emotions and memories, demands of us no action. It stays so far removed from objects that it is but the shadow of an illusion.

With the plastic arts, the novel and the drama we draw nearer, at least in appearance, to reality. The artist often calls upon nature for his subject. A picture by Rembrandt represents men and things. To create his heroes Balzac uses real people. But neither Rembrandt nor Balzac seeks to produce a servile copy of reality. Their art is not that of trompe l'oeil or deception. On the contrary they project their own temperament onto the things described. A painting by Rembrandt, whether it represents a carpenter's bench, a philosopher's dwelling, or the room of a young man at his books, is always bathed in the same golden light. The place, the model matter little. "An admirable sunset on canvas is not a beautiful sunset; it is a great painter's sunset." *

The artist, Malraux goes on to say, has no call to submit to the world by means of a servile recording of it. He is not the transcriber of the world; he is its rival. His will to differentiate is as strong as his will to resemble. "What Rodin calls nature is what he takes from nature." Francis Bacon said that art was man added to nature. Yes, art is nature seen through one man's eyes, ordered by one man's mind, colored by one man's temperament.

This human order holds sway over all the arts. Like music, the dance follows rhythms and refined combinations of rhythms. Poetry, in every language, has rhythms peculiar to it. In some idioms it is a matter of the alternation of long and short (or stressed and unstressed) syllables, in others one of a regular number of syllables ending in repeated identical sounds, or rhymes. Sometimes a refrain will mark the end of each verse. Why do we enjoy this? Because we take pleasure in being on the alert, be it unconsciously, for the recurrence of rhythm or rhyme; because the poet submits the tragic passions to a discipline which soothes us. All the great orators, from Pericles to Cicero, from Lincoln to Churchill, were addicted to repetitions,

* Malraux.

to symmetry of phrase and to a crescendo in their exhortations.

In the plastic arts rhythms and themes take other forms. Every architect respects certain proportions, and repeats certain effects. An alignment of columns or of windows is the image of a simple rhythm. It can be made more complex by giving a new form to one window out of three, or out of five. Many monuments are symmetrically ordered with reference to a central point (in Paris, the Invalides and the Institut; in Rome, Saint Peter's; in Washington, the White House). Others on the contrary owe their unexpected charm to a happy disorder. The painter with the green of a dress matches the green of a meadow, he invents a splash of red or yellow which nature had not supplied, he orders his canvas with reference to its diagonal, creating a necessary alternation of our attention from side to side of this central line. He paints not what he sees, but what his mind demands. Renoir, with the sea at his feet, painted "Les Lavandières," the laundry maidens, bathing not in the sea but in a stream. Corot felt he had to put the final touches to a landscape, "The House," in his own studio. As to abstract painters, with them everything is arbitrary order. They paint their minds only.

In a novel a character, however complex, is infinitely more intelligible than an actual being. Madame Bovary undergoes profound changes in the course of her successive disappointments, but these changes are simpler by far than those of an actual woman. Proust created Swann, Charlus, Odette out of a small number of components. A human mind, be it that of the greatest novelist, cannot and should not reproduce life's infinite complexity. His role is to create an illusion while staying relatively simple.

This nice balance is difficult to maintain. If the composition is too readily intelligible, the spectator or the reader will not feel the illusion that it approaches nature. This will be serious indeed, since one of the pleasures afforded by art is just this illusion: that reality is made intelligible. So complexity must be simulated. Modern writers, as a result, particularly since Proust, Joyce and Faulkner, have been striving to maintain a certain measure of disorder by juggling with time and space, leaping back into the past and forward into the future as the thoughts of living beings would do. The art of our times tries to reintegrate into its ordered elements some of the disorder of things, some of their obscureness. The novelist of the new school takes pride in being difficult and in putting the mind of his reader to work.

He can do this all the more easily since one order necessarily pervades all an artist's works, the order which derives from the author's own temperament. We can recognize, almost unfailingly, that a work, a sentence even, is that of an artist with whom we are familiar. A lover of painting, visiting a gallery, will say from quite a way off: "There's a Cézanne, a Renoir, a Manet, a Mannessier." There is no mistaking Cézanne's palette and his method of construction, the fringes of light which surround Renoir's figures, the hard purity of Manet's contours. Imagine the same woman painted by Vermeer, Rubens and Watteau. The woman will be of no importance; you will have a Vermeer, a Rubens, a Watteau.

"Man adds to nature." We must ever revert to this formula. Every writer has within him certain themes by which his whole output will be permeated. We find in Balzac an *Arabian Nights* theme, partly because in childhood he had been entranced by this book, partly because, frustrated in his youth, he dreamed of the great wealth and the great loves that an enchanter, in the *Arabian Nights,* lavishes upon his hero. We find in the elder Dumas a theme of the Righter of Wrongs, of the strong man who intervenes, when injustice threatens, to ensure the triumph of justice. In Baudelaire we find a theme of exotic travel, a theme of debauchery and a theme of death. In Proust, a theme of the flight of Time and of Time recaptured. All these men are the greater for having given rein to their temperaments. A second-rate writer paints things as he knows they are, not as he actually sees them. "That alone can be beautiful which bears the seal of our choice, of our taste, of our uncertainty, of our desires and of our frailty," says Proust. This attitude is the opposite of that of the scientist, who on the contrary seeks not to perceive in things his own desires and his own weakness. The laws of Kepler express neither Kepler's joys nor his sorrows.

We could, with respect to science, reverse Bacon's definition and say: "Science is man withdrawn from nature." We may take an interest in the personality and the life of a man of science, but we should be astonished and shocked were his personality and his life to oblige him to modify the results of his observation. When we read Einstein or Heisenberg we do not expect to detect, in their operations and their reasoning, like the watermark in the paper of a printed page, the man Einstein or the man Heisenberg, with their defects, their virtues and their desires. But, on the contrary, we are grateful to Victor Hugo for being Victor Hugo in his every word; we are grateful to Chagall for being Chagall in a stained glass window as in a ceiling; we do not complain if the artist presents us with distorted images. These are the images we expect from him.

On the stage we do not demand of Shakespeare, of Molière an accurate picture of human life. We know, we feel, that King Lear, that Lady Macbeth are extreme cases such as we shall rarely, and perhaps never, meet. We know, we feel, that human beings are not quite so ridiculous as Molière paints them. But such exaggeration disturbs us not at all. That is just what we came to see. The exaggeration of horror or comedy helps us more easily to apprehend them. Not by putting before our eyes a scene designed to reproduce total illusion; on the contrary the theatre does everything to scotch any such absolute illusion. The stage, high above us, the footlights, the scenery, actors who come back after their death to take their bows, all these factors separate the spectator from the spectacle, saying to him in chorus: "You are not living this, but what you see, just because you are not involved, will help you to understand life."

Yet the presence of certain elements of reality in a work of art is necessary. "Man added to nature." We have shown that man's personality and his intelligence as the creator of order are indispensable to a work of art. But nature is no less so. What gives us the feeling of beauty is to see a reality which we had failed to understand, suddenly yielding to the discipline of the mind. If this reality were totally absent, if we could find in the work of art no strong passions, no men, no women, none of those vague thoughts which haunt our daydreams, then we should become indifferent to the work. We have said that a crowd, subjected to the discipline of a ceremony, acquires beauty. True enough, but first you must have the crowd. A ceremony without a single onlooker would lose all grandeur. A poem is beautiful when strong passions have bowed to the yoke of rhythm and rhyme. A tragedy of Racine's reaches the sublime because its burning human emotions form such a contrast with the dignity and restraint of classical verse.

These strict rules have never embarrassed a great artist. He is stimulated by resistance. The unusual shapes of the blocks of marble entrusted to Michelangelo by his patrons and tyrants forced him to give his statues some unexpected attitudes, themselves forms of beauty. Both Shakespeare and Molière were obliged to write for specific troupes. This constraint imposed particular physical traits for a given role. How fortunate: Hamlet was short of breath because the actor Burbage, who was to play the part, was stout. This detail makes for a more living Hamlet. Molière often had to compose a play on the King's orders and at the shortest notice. A superficial critic would say: "Creating a masterpiece under such circumstances is impossible." The able critic will retort: "It is impossible to create a masterpiece without submitting to some kind of rule." Leonardo da Vinci taught that strength for an artist is born of constraint and perishes from freedom.

A novel elaborated by the sole play of the mind, in order to prove a thesis or to apply a technique of the novel, is never a great book. Illusion withholds itself from mere intelligence. The finest novels started out from nature. Tolstoy was inspired to write *War and Peace* by his family history; an actual trial inspired Stendhal for *The Red and the Black;* his own early years Dickens for *David Copperfield*. But the great artist transforms the data supplied by nature. Great art lives half way between primeval chaos and the dazzling radiance of intelligence. Mere chaos would be devoid of beauty, mere intelligence devoid of emotion. The greatest drama, that of Shakespeare, of Calderon, of O'Neill, yes and that too of Ionesco, of Beckett, is not without its share of folly. The modern cinema produces scarcely structured films, steeped in the wilful absurdity of surrealism. They retain a certain measure of beauty thanks to the choice of the images and to the recurrence of some of them which, in these poems on film, play the part of the rhyme or of the refrain. We take pleasure in a scene of extreme confusion subjected to the rule of an artist. We are grateful to Balzac for having created a world, because in this world, made by the hand of a craftsman, we can move about more at our ease than in the real world, while yet finding in Balzac's a variety which gives us the illusion of reality.

Here we must face a difficult question. We have just said "the illusion of reality," but what is reality for an artist? It cannot be everything that our senses perceive. A novelist creates a hundred, a thousand characters. In the real world there are billions. The artist must choose. He will select certain types, certain rich occasions. Beyond things themselves he will seek for the mysterious secret they hold and hide. Indeed just as in science the researcher modifies particles by his observation of them, so the artist exercises an influence upon the so-called real world. If Tolstoians exist it is because of Tolstoy. The eroticism of the novelists and the film makers of the twentieth century is breeding an actual eroticism. After Goethe had written *Werther,* real men committed suicide.

So the artist, in part, *creates* reality. He teaches us to see, and to see ourselves. Bergson has shown that we, the civilized, stand in need of the re-education of our senses. The habit of thinking in words is so deeply engrained in us that we no longer know how to see or to hear. We recognize labels, not realities. We say: "England . . . France . . . the Americans. . . ." Buried beneath these words lies a vast wealth of complex facts. To say: "The Americans are this way, or that way" can scarcely be called a thought. There is no such thing as "*the* Americans." There are Americans. We declare: "He is in love with that woman," but life refuses any such summing up. Life is full of delicate shadings, of contrasts. To love . . . why there are thousands of ways of loving.

Under the cover of his words the great novelist sets forth on a search for life. The beauty of a landscape often stays unnoticed by those who dwell nearby until such time as a painter of genius divests it of its veils. Monet, Sisley, Pissarro literally *created* the beauty of the Marne and the Seine, Utrillo that of the white walls of the back streets of Paris. "Only through art can we step out of ourselves, and know what another may be seeing in this universe which is not the same as ours." Art corrects the ill effects produced by our pride and our abstract intelligence. It forces us to plunge into the depths, to go beyond words. In the official bulletins World War I was devoid of reality; a handful of novelists succeeded in investing it with that reality. Their illusion has become our truth.

Once more: What is reality? Writers have such difficulty in answering this question that, generation after generation, they have claimed that they were more realistic than their predecessors. In France the romantics (Victor Hugo, Musset) accused the classical authors of using an abstract vocabulary which no longer embraced any part of reality. Thirty years later the naturalists (Zola and his disciples) indicted the romantics for their lack of realism. Had naturalism, then, at last reached reality? Not at all. Proust showed that real emotions are as far removed from conventional emotions as is the microscopic from the macroscopic world. But Proust himself depicted characters, personalities. The new wave of novelists (Robbe-Grillet, Nathalie Sarraute) pride themselves on exercising no choice. As disciples of Joyce, they set down the tritest remarks, describe the most insignificant characters, interpret silences. In the eyes of the new novelist there lies reality. "In life," he will say, "there is rarely any story. Life is commonplace. We must paint the daily run of things and paint it in disorder, for reality is disordered."

To tell the truth it is not a matter, for the artist, of reproducing an unattainable reality, which in any case is not the object of art, but rather of constructing *his own* reality, using the elements afforded to him by life, by his own thoughts, and imposing the illusion of order. It is not a matter of the artist's seeing properly, but rather dreaming properly. If he can give us both the illusion of remaining in a real world and the illusion of suddenly understanding this world, then he has fulfilled his duty which is, as Aristotle said of old, "the catharsis of passions." For the main source of distressing passions, the greatest foe to peace of mind is imagination. As soon as we are at rest, with nothing to focus our attention, our imagination wanders off *into the future or into the past.* In our future it reveals dangers, diseases and disappointments—in love, in our profession or in our friendships. In our past it resurrects our mistakes in order to correct them. "Ah yes," we say to ourselves, "if that one time I had told him frankly all that I had on my mind, everything might have been different." And we spend distressing days and nights in sorrowful and fruitless meditation.

How can we soothe our imagination? By focusing our attention upon scenes which that imagination cannot transform. Illusions? Yes, but durable illusions, fraught with no dangers. We can indulge in daydreams about Madame Bovary, but all that we shall ever know of her is already in Flaubert's novel. We do not try to convince her, to save her. Why, we have, for years, known all the endings of our favorite books. When we reread *War and Peace,* we know that the delightful Natacha will become a staid matron. When we go to see Shakespeare's *Julius Caesar* we *know* that the dictator is doomed and that he will fall under the conspirators' daggers. This very certainty contributes to our serenity and to our happiness. We *know* that Vermeer's girl with a turban will stay the same, whatever we may say or do. The face of a real woman changes like an April sky and we seek in vain in her expression the key to our fate; but the Mona Lisa's equivocal smile is immutable. With respect to the drama or to paintings we have no decisions to take. When we gaze upon them our imagination can, and in fact must, come to rest. The spectator at the play has come to see fear, folly, pity. He knows that the tragic heroes will be the victims of their own passions, or of Fate. And yet he finds pleasure in this. Why? Because at last, in life's drama, he is a spectator and not an actor.

This brings up an important question, one which is often misunderstood. Since the reader (or the spectator) seeks in a work of art a refuge where he may feel freed from the duty of taking action or passing judgment, will this work of art not be spoiled if it imposes the moral judgments of the author? Chekhov once wrote: "When I describe horse thieves, there are people who would like me to say that it is wicked to steal horses. But that is none of my business; that is up to the courts." He was right. Any explicit moral is harmful to a work of art. When Tolstoy preaches in his own name he is less great than when he lets Peter Bezoukhow or Levine point his moral. The moral must be inherent in the work itself and not in the wisdom of the author. Carlyle's biographies are less fine than Lytton Strachey's because Carlyle cannot refrain from sermonizing his characters. "Surely poor Louis XV could have been allowed to die without a homily from Chelsea." But all great works do contain an implicit moral, a view of the world which transpires through the events and the characters. It is undeniable that, after reading a great novel, after seeing a fine play, after hearing a splendid concert, we feel purified. We have understood that Time changes all things, that compared to the tragedy of a great sorrow, our little daily mishaps are of very slight importance. We have learned to recognize as our brothers and sisters men and women unknown to us. In short we have become better.

We can now sum up what the illusions of art bring to man, and why we cultivate them. We have seen that art is a substitute for action when action is impossible; we have seen that art introduces intelligible order into the representation of anarchic nature; we have seen that art reveals facets of reality which had escaped our notice; and lastly we have seen that art soothes our imagination by supplying it with what life constantly refuses: "the merging of contemplation and action." In all these respects, art differs from science.

There are a few further differences, and they are fundamental. (1) The scientist's study of nature results in information which will immediately be translated into techniques. Science has made possible the telephone, television, aviation, nuclear energy. In short, science is useful. Pure research itself has always, sooner or later, and involuntarily, resulted in practical applications. Art, on the contrary, is no begetter of techniques other than that of the artist himself, an individual technique which can be of scant use to others. Ask a great painter: "How do you do it?" He will answer: "If I knew, I should not be doing it."

(2) The scientist seeks to sharpen his critical faculties; the artist leaves his dormant. He does his best work in a state of grace and rapture which he tries to provoke now through love, now through isolation, now by means of an exotic life, scornful of all conventions, now by means of stimulants: coffee, hashish, peyotl. He tries to escape from the real world; he is not of that world. Be he impassioned, be he absent-minded, the scientist must still be part of that world in order to submit it to his experiments.

(3) Science progresses. An idea or a theory which used to seem the best makes way for others, newer and more apt to explain phenomena. Art never progresses. Proust does not replace Balzac; Racine is not an improvement over Sophocles; Joyce does not eliminate Dickens. Praxiteles cannot make us forget the genius of the Egyptian sculptors. T.S. Eliot reports a conversation. The first interlocutor, a man of scientific training, says:

"The writers of the olden days are far removed from us because we know so much more than they did." His friend replies: "Precisely, and that *more* is nothing other than our knowledge of them." * So much for the differences.

Yet we must come back to that saying of Einstein's: "The man of science and the poet are brothers." Let us take a closer look at this. Why does a man become an artist? We have said that man has recourse to representation when he is debarred from action, or finds it difficult. In almost every artist we find, at the outset, a difficulty in adapting which inspires him with the desire of escaping from the real world, in order to express an imaginary one. Byron was lame. Victor Hugo came from a broken home; his family was afflicted by hereditary insanity. Dickens underwent a youth of pure horror, steeped in shame and poverty. Balzac suffered from an infantile trauma. Jean Cocteau never ceased being obsessed by his father's suicide. Proust was sensitive to the point of neurosis. These disorders often stay unnoticed because, if he succeeds in producing a masterpiece, the artist finds release and may, quite early in his life, emerge as a happy and triumphant individual. But had he not suffered he would not have triumphed. Suffering, for an artist, is the midwife of genius.

So we have a man, keenly sensitive, rich in memories because the impressions of his childhood and his youth were so strong, who finds himself cast upon the universe. He observes what is happening around him and, particularly, within him. He both senses and knows that his vocation is to write, to paint or to compose music. But what shall he write, how shall he paint?

* Quoted by Justin O'Brien.

This he does not know, and no intellectual effort will tell him. Then, all of a sudden, when he least expects it, after reading a book, in the course of a conversation, during a sleepless night, his mind is flooded by radiant certainty. In a flash he sees the works to come. In the case of Balzac, for instance, a first illumination: The historical novel is in vogue, European readers are passionately devouring Walter Scott. Why should not he, Honoré de Balzac, write novels of the contemporary scene, with the same structure as historical novels? Today his idea seems simple and even commonplace. In those days it was quite new and was the starting point of his entire production. The second illumination, just as sudden, just as fleeting, a few years later: Why not link all my novels together in one single picture of our times, with constantly recurring characters? At that very instant *The Human Comedy* was born. So Proust, after a long but fruitless search for the form to be given to a novel in which he could express all his oppressions, after having knocked on every door to free that captive beauty, came by chance upon an invisible door which instantly, spontaneously, swung open and proved to be the right one. He had suddenly understood that the subject of his novel was to be that novel itself, and the transmutation of Things Past into Things Recaptured.

These examples allow us to understand why Einstein said to Saint-John Perse: "The man of science and the poet are brothers." For the scientist too starts out from a sudden intuition which is like the metaphor of a poet. Newton sees the apple fall and says to himself that the moon is a huge fruit falling to Earth. Every man of science, pursuing the dream of a hypothesis, follows the same mental process as the artist. The difference is that the scientist, having, at one radiant glimpse, and by some stroke of genius conceived his hypothesis, then submits it to the test of experiments; while the writer must nourish, out of his memory and his observations, the subject of which he has just caught the first glimpse. His swift illumination has supplied him with a theme, perhaps with characters. He now has to bring these to life. To carry this out successfully the author will toss into his crucible human beings he has met, but he will distort and magnify them. Naturally he will also toss in a great deal of himself. He seeks to recover the illusions of his childhood, for he depends upon them to add the most personal elements to his vision. The gap between the illusions of youth and the disillusions of old age, endless errors endlessly corrected: that, indeed, is life. The finest, perhaps the only, subject of a novel is "Lost Illusions." Balzac wrote this novel, but so did Goethe, with *Wilhelm Meister,* so did Sartre, with *Words,* and Dickens too, with *David Copperfield,* and Stendhal throughout all his works.

So we see that if for the scientist and for the artist the starting place is the same—a sudden intuition—their subsequent labors diverge sharply. For the artist it is a matter of rediscovering sensitive impressions, unrevised by intellect; for the scientist a matter of erasing every last vestige of subjectivity. "A painting is the best possible image of the painter," says Picasso. Even abstract art, which does its best to eliminate the slightest trace of figurative life, even informal art, throwing onto the canvas its violent and haphazard splashes of color, reveal the artist and his nature. Irrepressible human thought seeps out between the geometrical, crisscross lines and from among the vehement, elementary colors. Art is the operation thanks to which thoughts that, otherwise, would have remained private phenomena become the matter of possible communication, not only between man and man, but between generations, between centuries and tens of centuries. We read Homer, and in his works we can identify man as we identify him in the statues of Egypt or of the Incas. Art creates lasting illusions; science dispels fleeting illusions.

But these divergences do not imply conflict between the certainties of science and the illusions of art. Certainties and illusions are complementary. The discoveries of science, its excursions into the realms of the infinitely small and the infinitely great are, for the poet, subjects of wonder and of awe. Electricity inspired one of Dufy's masterpieces. And the scientist, in turn, needs poetry, music, paintings, to approach something which is as much a part of the universe as a magnetic field or as particles, something which can be neither defined nor measured, but the existence of which we cannot help feeling in the very depths of our mind.

It is probably extremely rare for a great scientist to be a great musician or a great painter. To reach a high degree of perfection in a science or in an art, the subject must be totally devoted to his chosen discipline. But there is nothing to stop the physicist from loving music, the chemist from loving painting, the biologist from loving literature. I shall even venture to say that there is a very good chance of the scientist's understanding the arts and taking pleasure in them, this for four reasons. First because he is a man; next because he is a man of exceptional intelligence, which helps him to fathom art's mysterious symmetry; next because he discovers esthetic values in the symmetries and the structures of nature and even in those of mathematical operation; and last because, after having spent his day in austere research far beyond our human dimensions, he more than anyone else must take pleasure in reverting to the eternal concepts and the vast contradictions inseparable from man's estate. Einstein said that the deepest and finest emotion we are capable of feeling is the sensation of mysticism. The scientist respects the radiant beauty of works of art; the artist likes to dream of the infinities revealed'to him by the man of science.

There remains one practical problem: Can art subsist in a world ruled by science and technology? What reasons are there for fearing that such survival may be difficult or impossible? A first reason could be that science, with its precise measurements and its objectivity, might destroy the illusions from which the fine arts take their being. But we have already said that science, to this day, is still very far from embracing and explaining human passions. Furthermore, how could science destroy the illusions of the artist, since both he and his audience *know* that illusions *is* what they are? The most ingenious theories of light take nothing away from Rembrandt or Van Gogh. On the contrary, the impressionist painters were actually guided by some degree of scientific knowledge as to the nature of light.

A second cause for alarm: Would we not be right in thinking that new techniques (the radio, television, films, "hi-fi" platters and tape recorders) will allow man to do without the arts, other means of escape being now available? Will motion pictures and television not satisfy that need of fictitious adventure which used to provide readers for the novel and audiences for the stage? At first glance it would appear to me that the new techniques of the mass media more probably help artists to reach wider audiences. A play broadcast over television will be seen in villages, in lonely farms where never a show of any kind was ever seen before. In one single evening Sophocles, Shakespeare, Molière now reach more spectators than they had reached over the centuries. The greatest music can be heard by millions of listeners. Motion pictures seize upon a famous novel, such as *Anna Karenina* or *The Charterhouse of Parma* and show the filmed version to crowds the world over. Yes, but. . . .

But is it possible to preserve on the screen the emotions and the ideas which gave its value to the book? Obviously not. A show lasts two hours, which squeezes a vast epic into a very few scenes. What gives a book its spiritual value is that we can re-read it, turn back to an earlier chapter, ponder at length over a single page. Neither the motion picture nor television allows such study in depth. The television viewer does not cooperate so actively as the reader. To this one may retort that films are recruiting sergeants for readers. In the course of the weeks immediately following the screening of *War and Peace* in France, three hundred thousand copies of the novel were sold. The stage seems, for our new techniques, even more readily transposable, since the length of the two types of shows is approximately the same. However the unity of place is less acceptable on film or on television than on the stage, where the audience puts up with the monotony of the images because the presence of live actors imbue the production with human warmth. Motion picture techniques demand frequent and rapid changes; they have, in fact, transmitted this requirement to contemporary plays and novels. Is this a bad thing? Not at all, it is a mutation.

Color television is a priceless aid to painting. The masterpieces of our galleries can be brought to every hearth and home. To be sure, nothing can replace the actual painting. But here too the wish to get to know the work of the artist is fostered by the reproductions. As to music, recordings today are so highly perfected that the most sensitive lover of music can, in his own home, enjoy all the pleasures of the concert, with the sole exception of sharing them with others. It has been said that the techniques of the mass media, just because they must appeal to all, necessarily fall below the quality level which more restricted audiences used to demand. This is not unavoidable. No doubt if television and radio aim at catering to the most vulgar tastes, they will debase cultural levels. But radio, television, in the hands of men who, on the contrary, aim at developing education and culture may very well impose a higher level. Great passions, noble passions interest the masses as well as the élite. The masses admire courage, love, friendship, motherhood. The élite only too often tend to scorn such strong, permanent emotions, in favor of vogues. It would be quite possible to count on the support of popular audiences for the perpetuation of the old masterpieces and the creation of new ones. But first there must be the will to do so.

Another objection: Thanks to modern mass media techniques, thanks to communication satellites, we are present at every point of our planet where an event may be occurring. We can actually see those millions of young Chinese, fanatically flourishing the *Thoughts of Mao;* we are in the thick of battle among the Vietnam rice paddies; we can hear the voices of Negroes and Whites in Rhodesia. How can one hope to hold the attention of audiences so surfeited with the exotic? How can an artist expect to recapture the fresh luster of folklore which, in earlier days, astounded and fascinated readers and spectators alike? For that matter, how can the original characteristics of nations survive when the trend is toward the establishment of a universal scientific civilization? Are the fine arts not in danger of perishing for lack of raw materials?

Here too I think it is relatively easy to find the answer. (1) We are still far removed from that total entropy of emotions which, in an international community, would abolish all original ways of life. Seville is not like Tokyo; Paris is like neither London nor New York. (2) Our times spread before the artist a new world, there to be painted. The thought of youth today is conditioned by speed, space, musical backgrounds, aerodynamics, relativity. "The view from the roof terraces of Orly Air Field is a stirring sight for our younger generation," writes the physicist Leprince-Ringuet. "The swift vision of Paris, with its thousands of bright dots, ordered like the holes in some vast display of punch cards" extends before the young a modern version of the picturesque, ready for its poet. (3) The writer's original contribution is not the folklore, it is his own personality. The more monotone society may become, the more eagerly will the human mind listen to the outpouring of personal and moving strains of music. The mission of the writer, the painter, the film maker is to animate things, to imbue them with his sensitivity and thus to awaken that of readers and audiences. And this mission is unchanged; it is more urgent than ever before.

We shall perhaps see the emergence of a new kind of artist. There is a place in the world of the future for young men, writing especially for television and directing their own works. Would these be ephemeral? Not necessarily, and besides, what would this matter? Is a work which stirs the emotions of thirty million human beings in one single evening not as important as one which stirs one million in the course of three centuries?

Some modern artists will rely on uncertainty and on chance. A mobile by Calder is not a fixed, immovable work; it owes its beauty in part to the artist, in part to the winds that blow, in part to light. Some are on the alert for the *happening,* the unforeseeable event which will never recur: the audience joining in the play; the reader recomposing a book deliberately disjointed by the author; action painting. The refrain is no longer that of Poe's *Raven:* "Never more," but "Never again." I do not believe that this form of art will do away with the arts we have loved, whose beauty, power and necessity remain intact; but who knows? Perhaps the new forms will afford us moments of great enjoyment. We should neither neglect nor belittle them.

The new techniques also produce quite curious secondary effects. Not so long ago orators and singers could be heard without the help of a microphone. They no longer can, today, partly because they are accustomed to this accessory organ, but principally because audiences have become used to noise. Over the radio as on television the listener has only to twist a knob to increase the volume. The modern world enjoys tumult. A jazz combo with its electric guitars makes a great deal more noise than a symphony orchestra. In bars and cafés the customers live in the midst of the most alarming din. In the nineteenth century poets sought for silence and for shade where they might dream their dreams; many students, today, cannot work without background music. The same is true of light. We have become accustomed to enormous lighting power. Lighted as it used to be, a stage would seem dark to us now. This excessive light is bad for the eyes, but the instinct has been acquired and we shall not reverse the trend, at least not in civilization as we know it.

There is another instrument which exerts an influence on literature—the tape recorder. It makes available to the novelist or to the biographer conversations and narrations in the raw, with all their hesitations, their meanderings, their long-winded passages and their repetitions. Naturally such tapes do not form a work of art. The artist must subject them to *his* unity, must exert a choice, must give them a style. But they do provide him with his raw materials. One gets the impression that Salinger's short stories owe something to the technique of the tape recorder, even if this author does not actually use one.

The influence of these techniques, I repeat, by no means prevents the birth of the illusions of art. The danger for the fine arts does not stem from science. Science has perhaps been responsible for a shrinkage of the mental area within which illusions are possible. But the essence of what, since men have been men, has represented the matter of art still persists. An emotional or a passionate equation includes so great a number of variables that no computer, not even the best of them, can resolve it. To cast light upon such subjects as these we must revert to the traditions which have helped men to steer their course among the reefs and shallows of life, we must read the historians, the philosophers, the novelists, the poets; we must study the humanities if we wish to understand human affairs. Science is a wonderful instrument for the discovery of what may be known of the real world. Art is a refuge where the contemplation of an imaginary world is possible.

Have we the right to seek refuge in illusions? Is it not of greater importance to modify the world in which we live? But love of the arts is by no means equivalent to a flight from our responsibilities in this real world. On the contrary, when we win a host of invisible friends—the great painter, the great writer, the great musician—we increase our strength for action and for discovery. After having lived for a few hours on the high peaks of art, on the morrow men return to their labors in the plains, refreshed, rejuvenated, ready for the struggle, ready for research. Watch the faces as you leave a superb concert. Strangers exchange smiles because they have just shared a great emotion. They have drawn closer because they have partaken, together, of "anger, love and forgiveness; of action and repose; of fear and trembling, tears and regrets; of farewells, absence and returns. More than one of them recognized himself and weeps." Illusions? Yes, indeed. But these illusions are the stuff of which our life is made.